THE BEST MEDICAL
ADVERTISING AND GRAPHICS
SELECTIONS FROM THE RX CLUB SHOWS

THE BEST MEDICAL
ADVERTISING AND GRAPH

SELECTIONS FROM THE RX CLUB SHOWS

ROCKPORT PUBLISHERS · ROCKPORT, MASSACHUSETTS
DISTRIBUTED BY NORTH LIGHT BOOKS · CINCINNATI, OHIO

STAFF

Art Director
Stephen Bridges

Book Designer
Dick Emery
Richard Emery Design

Editor
Joseph Fatton

Production Manager
Barbara States

Copyright © 1992 by Rockport Publishers, Inc.
All rights reserved. No part of this book may be reproduced in any form without written permission of the copyright owners. All images in this book have been reproduced with the knowledge and prior consent of the artists concerned and no responsibility is accepted by producer, publisher or printer for any infringement of copyright or otherwise, arising from the contents of this publication. Every effort has been made to ensure that credits accurately comply with information supplied.

First published in the United States of America by:
Rockport Publishers, Inc.
146 Granite Street
Rockport, Massachusetts 01966
Telephone: (508) 546-9590
Fax: (508) 546-7141
Telex: 5106019284 ROCKORT PUB

Distributed to the book trade and art trade in the U.S. and Canada by:
North Light, an imprint of
F & W Publications
1507 Dana Avenue
Cincinnati, Ohio 45207
Telephone: (513) 531-2222

Other Distribution by:
Rockport Publishers, Inc.
Rockport, Massachusetts 01966

ISBN 1-56496-025-0

10 9 8 7 6 5 4 3 2 1

Printed in Hong Kong

CONTENTS

Introduction / 7
Essays / 8

1 **Space Advertising / 17**

2 **Direct Mail / 79**

3 **Sales Promotion / 109**

4 **Posters / Displays / 179**

5 **Editorial / 191**

6 **OTC / Consumer / 225**

About the Rx Club / 234
Indexes / 236

INTRODUCTION

MEDICINE ON MADISON

About a hundred years ago, it was the heyday of the era of Patent Medicines. Advertisers could have made any claim, used any graphic and with their various nostrums, philtres, potions, pills, gizmos, and gadgets they could claim a cure for any disease, symptom, or ailment (real or imaginary) from abscesses to zoacanthosis. In 1906 Congress passed the Pure Food and Drug Act; with the passage of that act, in effect, modern medical, pharmaceutical, and healthcare advertising was born.

Today the fields of pharmaceutical and medical advertising and publishing are unique unto themselves. With few exceptions, there is not another venue that places greater demands on "product knowledge" while at the same time places constraints ranging from federal regulations to corporate regulatory policies. Despite these constraints, there is an entire industry of people whose jobs it is to create this type of advertising. Be creative. Ironically, that is both the challenge and the goal of pharmaceutical and medical advertising and publishing: to be creative within the confines of a highly technical and regulated environment.

In order to create a successful piece, you need only to remember a few simple points: know the product ... be aware of the regulatory environment ... identify the marketing objectives ... determine the product position...pay heed to the competitive environment ... target the audience ... find the right message ... select the right graphics (don't forget to make sure they work with the copy). And here's a quick checklist for a few more incidentals: design (die cuts, laser cuts, or interactive pieces?), Execution (should it be photographed or illustrated? solarized, varnished, or surprinted?), Typography (typeface: bold, serif or sans-serif and how does the kerning look?), Paper (will it break the book?), Ink (standard PMS colors or metallics?), and Production Quality; make sure that you have selected the right media vehicle. OK, you're half-way home. Next step is to insure that the piece gets noticed, is remembered, and accomplishes its marketing, sales, or tactical objectives. Piece of cake! It'sdone hundreds of times a day, thousands of times a year. Afterall, that's what creativity is, isn't it? Yes, and that's also partof the business of pharmaceutical, medical, and health-careadvertising.

By definition, creativity is virtually limitless. As you go through this book, remember that for every piece of work you see here, there are thousands of pieces you don't see. And practically every creative piece may have been preceded by 5, 50, or 100 other concepts and or executions — that fact alone is eloquent testimony to the knowledge, imagination and creativity of those within this industry and especially those whose works appear herein.

Introduction and the section introductions were written by Caren Spinner. Ms. Spinner is VP, Associate Creative Director, Copy at Vicom/FCB in San Francisco.

THE IMPORTANCE OF PLANNING

Michael Lyons

In the normal course of any business endeavor, it is very important to have a plan. On a day-to-day basis in the pharmaceutical communications industry, we all recognize the importance of our clients' Research & Development and Marketing plans. Those companies with the most commitment to those equally important plans seem to fare well – year in, year out.

Likewise, those of us on the communications side need to formulate our plans accordingly. Generally, the planning of corporations and agencies is done or approved by groups of individuals. This process does not diminish the importance of any one team player. Each member of the group, or team, has to have his or her own plan, one for the present and one for the future. As individuals we have to ultimately choose a career path. This is often a very difficult decision, both personally and in advising others.

In my own case I procrastinated for a longer period than necessary, but gradually turned to art as everyone had been advising me to do for years. Thus, it was necessary to formulate what was at that point a totally theoretical plan. I was realistic enough to understand that this plan might have to be subsequently altered as time went on and circumstances changed, but at least I had a direction, and that was an important start.

The first major change in the plan came after starting my career in a small New York City ad agency. I soon realized that things were not as ideal as I had imagined them to be while still in school. People in the advertising business seemed to get fired on a regular basis, often without warning. This was an event that I witnessed early in my career when several artists were terminated two weeks before Christmas, just as their credit cards were probably stretched to the limit for family celebrations.

This event only strengthened my resolve to work harder to develop a portfolio of such quality that I would always be competitive in the marketplace. The one flaw in the plan was that a professional finished portfolio requires the acceptance and approval of several other people. These people very often have their own strong feelings regarding the advertising and creative messages put forth. Everyone involved in promoting a product, both on the client side and within the agency producing the communications materials, wants a superior creative product. That's where the crux of the problem lies. Throughout history some of the most important ideas, ideas that revolutionized our life-styles and society itself, have been rather basic, simple concepts in retrospect. Yet, these new ideas have often been met with scorn and derision. It is not surprising then that if one attempts a career of producing ideas, one had better develop a thick skin in a hurry, even though one might be a sensitive writer or artist.

Ideas, as exciting as they are when first viewed, are also frightening in that they require a commitment to the concept at hand. It takes a forthright, courageous person to accept and approve a unique idea upon first view. I have known a few such people in my experience and still view them with admiration. More often than receiving a quick approval on a novel idea, the tendency is to "sleep" on it, think it over, and analyze it to see if it meets all the necessary requirements.

After a few weeks, or even months, the impact of the new concept begins to feel a little old. It may be time to go back to the drawing board. In all fairness, I must confess that there are innumerable solutions to a creative problem and only rarely do we hit one so outstanding that it diminishes all others.

Actually, the approval process can become stuck even before the work leaves the agency. We've all been in the position of trying to anticipate the clients' response to a creative solution, whether it be someone else's work or our own. Invariably the questions raised during the presentation are the same ones we should have asked ourselves before the client meeting. If the work stands up to the tough questions we ourselves raise, then we'll be in a better position to defend it more logically.

Even though as creative people we feel more emotional about our work, we have to remember that the decision to run an expensive promotional campaign is essentially a business decision for most corporations. True, one hopes that our clients get excited and involved in our mutual communications efforts. However, in my own experience, I have never been able to sell my work based on the promise that it will win creative awards. That's not the province of our clients; their goal is to interest and involve the target audience, namely the healthcare professional.

Trying to combine messages of medical science with exciting words or beautiful graphics can pose a formidable task. Yet, that's the role we've chosen for ourselves. The most rewarding aspect of our jobs is to accomplish all of the above goals.

If I have a philosophy about advertising in general, it is that before one can be sold on a product, one should not be offended by the seller. The message should be delivered in a truthful, intelligent manner, and even if the audience cannot be sold, they should be left with a better impression of the product and its advertiser. I have on occasion bought stock in companies whose advertising messages were of such intelligence that I couldn't help but be impressed by them. This unfortunately leaves me with a rather meager portfolio of stocks. This is probably just as well, since I'm neither a good gambler nor a good loser.

As I said earlier, one should have a plan. There's no question that this plan must be questioned and reevaluated periodically. Even with optimal long- and short-range planning, we have only so much control over events.

Early in 1979, John Dorritie and I formulated a rather hurried plan to start an agency. Separately in our earlier career plans there had always been a vague idea of doing such a thing. Now because of a client/product conflict within our previous agency, we found ourselves with the opportunity to start a new business. Together with Al Nickel, and with much trepidation, we went about the necessities and legalities of setting up offices. Our goal was to establish an agency of outstanding creative product and, if this venture met with success, to share our success with our employees.

After signing a lease for office space and presenting the realtor with a check, we assumed we were eligible to move into our new offices. Wrong. We were summarily evicted and found ourselves relegated to a table at the Lantern Coffee Shop. With my layout pad concealed beneath the table, we were indeed a laughable new venture. We then took a suite at the Tudor Hotel for a few more days. One of our clients called to ask whether we were fighting over which soap opera to watch. It was indeed one of the many times during that first year that I questioned the sanity of our decision. Finally our lease was approved, and once inside our own offices, we formally embarked upon our new endeavor. It was a scramble, and I must confess that despite the success of our venture, it's been a scramble ever since. That seems to be the nature of our business. In 1991 the plan took on a major setback with the unexpected death of John Dorritie, a blow that in the past has been fatal to some agencies. Fortunately we have built a staff of highly qualified, motivated professionals, dedicated to seeing the plan thrive.

I am grateful to all who have given that extra effort and as we look to the future, we will continue to adjust to a changing environment.

Today, the whole healthcare system is under intense scrutiny, and as history has shown, things will be much different a year or two from now. This fact is what makes life and business interesting. As long as we recognize the need to constantly look ahead to anticipate the change, and indeed to shape it, we'll keep pace. So with that thought in mind, it's time to go back to the drawing board, knowing that nothing is more certain than change, and nothing more archaic than an inflexible plan.

Three ads created by the author at Dorritie Lyons & Nickel. Minipress, an antihypertensive agent that attempted a strategic move to position itself as starting therapy; Feldene, an antiarthritis agent that simulated the "feel" of sandpaper, and also the benefits of pain-free movement. Navane is an antipsychotic agent whose advertising the author created while at Sudler & Hennessy and which is today assigned to DL&N.

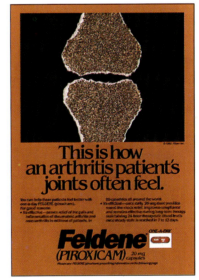

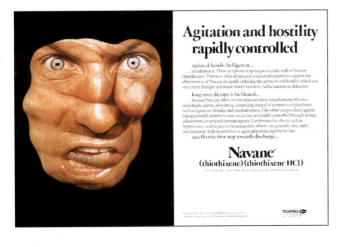

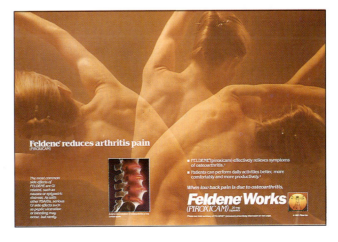

LIVE AND LEARN: THE WAY TO CREATIVITY

Michael Norton

In a *real* sense, this volume, filled with colorful visuals and words often as colorful, is a salute to the blank page and those who must fill it every day. Here we hold up for the world certainly to see, but moreover to study, the very best examples of creativity in healthcare advertising and promotion, as judged by those whose task it is to create and evaluate the work of others in their organizations.

Why? Can we teach creativity? Is it not a God-given talent?

Creativity can't be taught. Perhaps you'll recall the story of the musician who, when asked how to get to Carnegie Hall, responded: "Practice, practice, practice." Creativity is indeed a talent and, as such, cannot be taught; it is possible, though, with effort, to awaken the creativity in the "right side" of our brains — creativity that is often stifled in all of us. (Art Directors, look out! There are books that can teach copywriters how to draw; jobs are on the line here.) And it is possible to teach the *craft* involved in what we do — in one way by sharing the triumphs of the artisans of commercial endeavor, as exemplified here.

Perhaps the first step in the teaching process is an analysis of what others regard as good examples of creativity ... what you now hold in your hands.

No, we can't teach creativity, but we can teach how to recognize it. We can't give creativity as a gift, but we can make it available for the taking. We can't show how to create, but we can showcase the fruits of creativity, for appreciation, for stimulation, and to set a standard for others to reach, and perhaps to better. So while this book cannot be properly called a textbook in creativity, it most certainly serves as a creative tool.

Using experience, staying young. To me, creativity incorporates a need to remain "forever young." In terms of what we do as commercial persuaders, the reference is not to age, but rather to attitude. It means taking a forever-young approach to our work, at all times utilizing the experience we are continuously gaining, keeping our minds attuned to what's going on around us. In this way, we capture the astonishment, impulsiveness, unabashed "Why Not?" attitude that we brought to our business as bright-eyed beginners.

Laura Ingalls Wilder inscribed the insecurities of growing up to remain forever young when, at the age of 70, she first published Little House on the Prairie (her first book had been published five years earlier). Certainly Michelangelo took a fresh approach when, at 70, he began filling the cracks in the ceiling of St. Peter's Basilica. Verdi was a young thinker when he wrote Othello at 72, Flagstaff at 77. Sophocles taught generations how to make the complex simple when he wrote Oedipus Rex at 70, then Electra at 80. And while we don't know how old Moses was when he came down from the mountain, we know Cecil B. deMille was 75 when he gave us The Ten Commandments, in color.

Working at it. All of these young thinkers were, of course, inspired in some way. And while it's nice to think that they had all the time in the world to complete their commissions, as opposed to the deadline-driven world in which we work, I would venture that they too were attuned to time as an uncontrollable constraint.

They toiled to achieve what we might today call the "Wow!" effect. The chill, the eyebrow-raising physical manifestation of the inner experience we have when we view an endeavor — commercial or not — designed to capture our interests and convey a message. Who knows what served as inspiration for Ingalls Wilder, Michelangelo and the rest? But I'm sure they would have appreciated access to a compilation of the best in prairie navigation and ceiling restoration.

Those whose work is represented in these pages have toiled in the same way, to our enrichment, producing commercial work with the "Wow!" Sometimes it's been accomplished visually, sometimes with words alone. More often, it's the combination: art and copy together in that marriage or intimacy

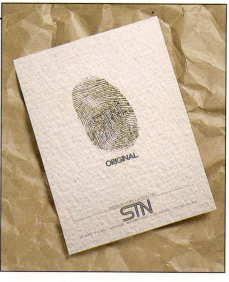

"Original" Ad. This self-promotional ad for Salthouse, Torre, Norton, Inc. uses a striking thumbprint incorporating the agency's logo with a one-word headline describing the agency's approach to creative and marketing problems. The ad is part of an award-winning series running since 1983.

that produces the orgasm of the mind that stimulates, yet leaves the reader rested, relaxed, refreshed in some way ... enriched, entertained, stimulated, jolted, and ready to consider, review, buy, sell, help, or take some other action that our words and pictures have intended to compel. Illustration, alliteration, and onomatopoeia (Wham! Bang!, the ADs know it when they see it). Calligraphy, photography, typography, and tone. Man and Mac-chines. Cursors and commas, one-ems and rhymes. They're all here, combined in a way that results in the "Wow!" effect. So look through these pages. Enjoy the talent and study the craft. If you don't experience that "Wow!", you may be dead. If you do experience it, there's more than a good chance that you will produce or cause to be produced the work that another generation will view with visceral effect ... Wow!

A noble theft. "Creativity is plagiarism undetected" (adapted from Anon.). We borrow from our experience and therefore owe it to ourselves to plagiarize from technology, from science, from art and music; to read, to see, to live, so

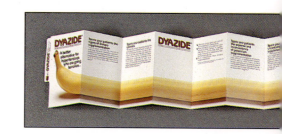

that it is reflected in the art form that is our business. In that sense, then, what you hold in your hands now is the textbook that can't be written, a reflection of the work inspired by the experiences and collaborations of the names in the credits, and hope for those who are working now for that flash of inspiration that will light the way to the next volume.

This work, and the ongoing work of the Rx Club in their annual exhibition, adds to the material from which we can find an unchartered track among the millions of neurons in the brain that fire into ideas. That's plagiarism, of course, but an enriching and noble plagiarism.

If you are one who must wrangle work through the wringer of reviewers, take heart that all of the work you see reproduced here has been through a similar process, whereby new parameters appear as if from nowhere, and views are as varied as the number of reviewers. Take heart, because it is possible to work within the parameters, interpretations, and other obstacles that arise. It is possible to remain forever young, without cosmetics. The proof is right here.

Left above, Dyazide "Bananas" Ad. "Never show the product in an ad directed at doctors." This ad breaks that rule, using the product itself in an entertaining way to make the same point that the file card does: the product controls blood pressure while preserving potassium loss that might otherwise have to be replaced, making patients go bananas!

Right above, Tagamet Ulcer Pain Ads. Graphics grab and words remind readers what this product does well. The result: recognition by readers (prescribers) and by the creative community (Rx Club judges). The layout is as simple as the message itself, and the compelling force is the familiarity with the imagery in the ads.

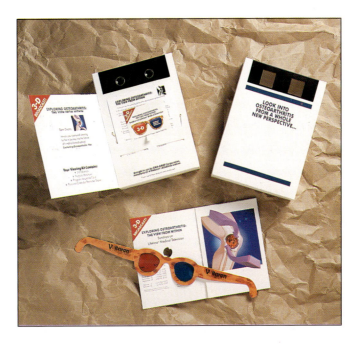

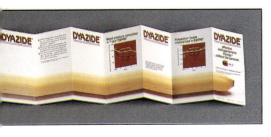

Above, Voltaren Promotion in 3-D. This "box" invites "viewers" to look into a debilitating arthritic condition from a whole new perspective — in this case the promotion (delivered by representatives and by mail) publicized the first 3-D television broadcast on medical television. In effect, the promotion was as creative as what was being promoted.

Left, **Dyazide File Card. Can a file card be creative?** The Rx Club judges gave this one a silver award for creativity. It competed against many "high-tech," big-budget visual aids and product brochures. The concept was the size of a potassium-rich banana (more than 3 feet!) that would have to be consumed to preserve the potassium spared by the product. Demonstration in print!

DANCING WITH WOLVES

Lewis E. Calver

What is this strange and puzzling creature? Does it have a language? First, get its attention. What is important to it? Does it not breathe? If words fail, try pictures.

In the mirror we see the truth: he is one of us, this physician, this scientist. And yet, what is he scribbling on that paper — that b.i.d, p.r.n.? And why does he seem to be in such a hurry?

We try to communicate with him. We have many reasons: self-satisfaction, pride, money. But how? Is he really different from us? What makes him unique?

As the creative team is formed to design communication, one of the most important elements - understanding - must not be overlooked. Certainly, this physician is human; he bleeds, he dreams. And yet he is a scientist. In this professional arena in which we have chosen to communicate, he is, above all else a scientist.

How does the world look through those science-colored glasses? Ideas are scrutinized for logic. Cleverness is judged in relation to the abstraction of scientific facts or principles. An otherwise aesthetic image is spoiled by needless inaccuracy. Communication is indeed judged on a much keener plane.

Medical illustrators have successfully bridged this communication gap. From Leonardo daVinci's clandestine dissections to the medical school biology and anatomy classes taken by today's medical illustration students, the key to success has always been understanding. Only when they are thoroughly knowledgeable on a subject can they employ accentuation, protraction, assimilation, and magnification necessary to effect true understanding.

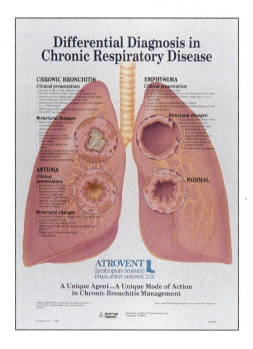

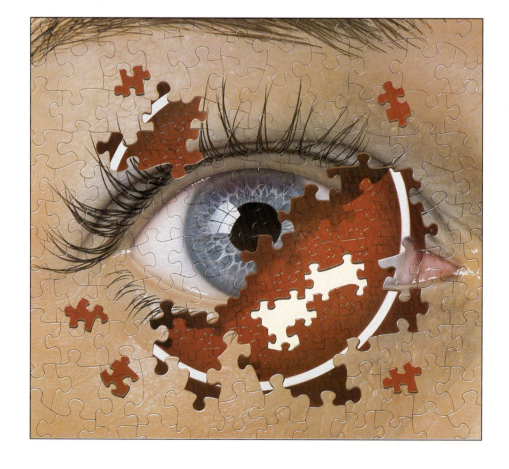

As the illustration student is "thrown in" with medical students to learn anatomy, histology, pathology, physiology, he also begins a career-long study of his clientele. Understanding the scientist, the audience, is equally important as the science.

When in the design process of communication is the medical illustrator, the interpreter, the guide, most valuable? The question seems to answer itself. Yet, the medical illustrator is usually called at the end with the familiar, " … and we need it next week." Maybe what is needed wasn't even considered or understood. How many campaigns are started, how many strategies conceived, without true understanding, without that critical bridge between communication, visualization, and science?

Do we dance or are we lunch?

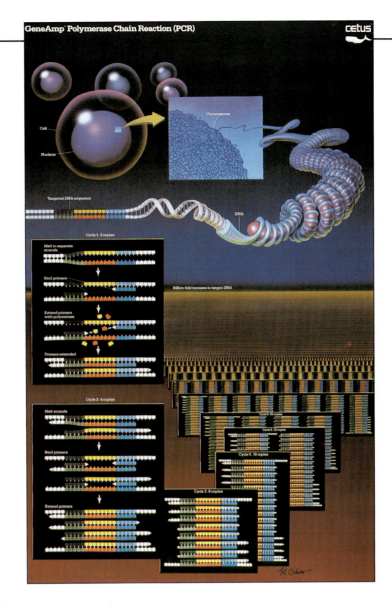

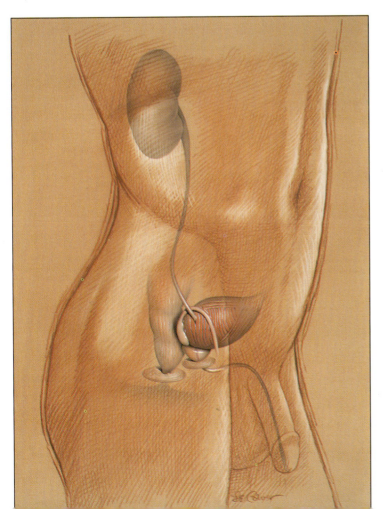

Clockwise from upper right

GeneAmp Polymerase Chain Reaction. A poster explaining a method of amplifying desired gene sequences from extremely small amounts of DNA, for Cetus Corp.

Urodynamics - Urethral and Anal Sphincters. Lead illustration for an article in *RN Magazine*.

Retina Puzzle. Limited edition print for The Retina Foundation of The Southwest.

Differential Diagnosis in Chronic Respiratory Disease. Poster for Boehringer Ingelheim Pharmaceuticals, Inc.

Structures Associated with the Limbic System in the Human Brain. Illustration for an article in *Newsweek*.

A FUNNY THING HAPPENED ON MY WAY TO THE STUDIO

By Carl Fischer

Except for the absence of Novocaine and *The New York Times*, had some advantages to the artist living in medieval times compared to the artist living today. In that earlier day, a carver or a stained-glass maker was as necessary to society as a baker or a carpenter, and his work was highly valued.

As an ordinary member of the community, he was not treated differently than any other worker, and more important, he did not consider himself any different. There was no fine art in the Middle Ages — all art was commercial art. It must have been a less stressful environment in which to work. Except, of course, for The Plague.

Today, fine artists are a unique, often distrusted class, and their art is viewed with suspicion or neglect. Mostly art is considered a cosmetic addition to our lives, an embellishment that we can do without, if necessary. That is a great loss. So much hoopla and so much public relations attends being an artist today that the stress to provide something unique, arcane, or outrageous pressures fine artists to provide work that panders to an enigmatic market. Add to that an artist's reputation as an abstruse person, plus the hyperbole that artists themselves like to engage in, and life can become a staggering burden.

That's why I am satisfied with the current state of commercial art, which somewhat parallels the role of the arts in the Middle Ages. Salaried artists do not have tenured employment, nor are they given grants in financial aid, but they are offered exhilarating opportunities in which to work. For an artist, work is the bottom line. True, much of the work that wins awards (including my own) in the cacophony of exhibitions often is not the most worthy. True, the proportion of good to bad in commercial art is a great deal of bad to very little good — perhaps the same proportion as in fine art, politics, or automobile repair. But that is another subject, isn't it?

An advantage of doing unsanctioned commercial art, rather than established fine art, is that commercial art is an important ingredient of our culture. It is widely understood and appreciated without the need for art appreciation courses or esthe65tic diagnosis. The artist can therefore eschew notoriety and can develop within a system that regards him as a necessary producer of useful things, not as a melancholy outsider.

No one has been able to show that the Bohemian life has produced work of a more lasting nature than that of the unknown piece-workers of Chartres, say, who did not feel constrained to sign their work. (It has been suggested that the masons who did sign their work during the building of St. Sophia did so in order to get paid.) Andy Warhol's drawings of shoes for Andrew Geller advertising were as good as anything he did for an art gallery.

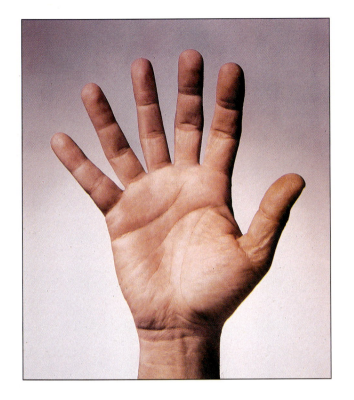

Commercial art has been abused, because it can make artists economically comfortable: a hopelessly middle-class failing. But Herbert Muller has written that "Plumbing is not necessarily fatal to the good life, or poverty or misery essential to spiritual elevation." Or, as Tevye has said, more wistfully, "It is not a great shame to be poor. On the other hand, it's not a great honor, either."

My experience in the business end of advertising has been sanguine: I have not seen the predatory behavior that is endemic in the garment and the entertainment businesses. Compared to them, working in advertising is like working in a monastery.

Which was another clever medieval invention.

1

SPACE ADVERTISING

Creative advertising — the ability to take a blank piece of paper and turn it into a vehicle of communication and persuasion. In this section you will see an array of ads across all therapeutic areas. All are highly creative and innovative solutions to sales and marketing challenges. Sometimes this is achieved through poignancy or drama, sometimes through amusement or humor. Others ads may educate, compel, or frighten. What they all have in common is that they are examples of outstanding advertising. When an ad stands out it does what an ad is supposed to do: be noticed, be remembered, communicate and sell.

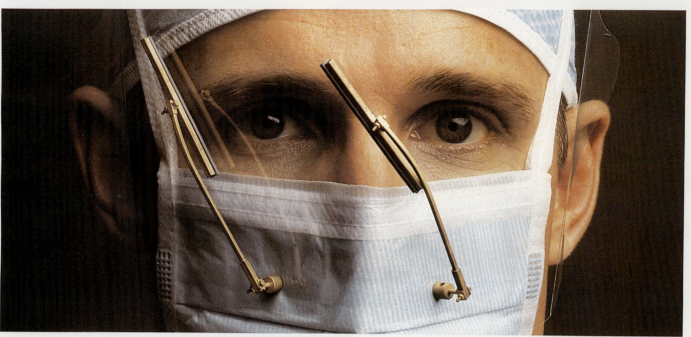

Product: **Extra Protection Face Mask**
Title of Graphic: **Protection So Complete**
Ad Agency: **Pierce-Davis & Associates**
Client: **Johnson & Johnson Medical, Inc.**
Art Director: **Pam Gampper, Jennifer Hope**
Photographer: **John Katz**
Copywriter: **Margie Bowles**
Stuctural Design: **Joseph Melancon**

Space Advertising

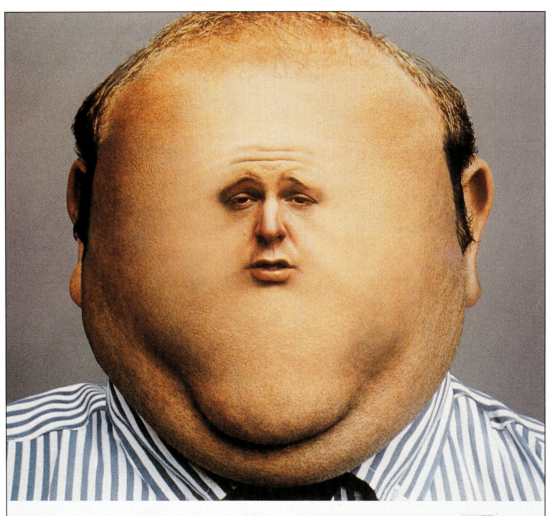

Product: **Benadryl**
Title of Graphic: **Deflate Nasal Congestion**
Ad Agency: **Sudler & Hennessey**
Client: **Parke-Davis, Consumer Health Product Group**
Art Director: **Ernie Smith**
Illustrator: **Jules Galian**
Photographer: **Ken and Carl Fischer**
Copywriter: **Sandra Holtzman**

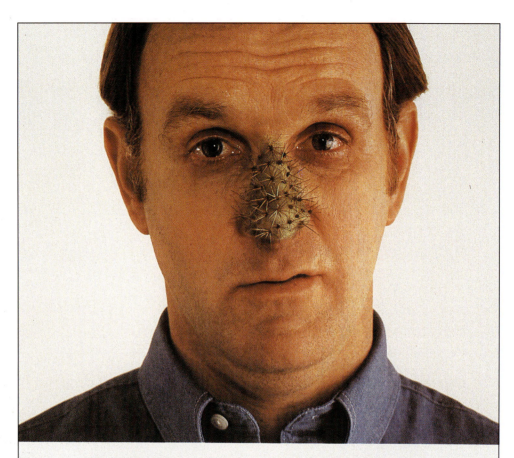

Product: **Guaifed**
Title of Graphic: **Cactus Nose**
Ad Agency: **Girgenti, Hughes, Butler & McDowell**
Client: **Muro Pharmaceuticals**
Art Director: **Scott Frank**
Photographer: **Brian Goble**
Copywriter: **Bob Ranieri**

Space Advertising

Product: **Feldene**
Title of Graphic: **It Helps Make Arthritic Joints More Articulate**
Ad Agency: **Dorritie Lyons & Nickel**
Client: **Pfizer Pharmaceuticals**
Art Director: **Mike Lyons**
Copywriter: **Bill Brown**

Product: **Monitor One**
Title of Graphic: **Issues in Ischemia**
Ad Agency: **Cline, Davis & Mann, Inc.**
Client: **Q-Med**
Art Director: **Tom Zalewski, Andy Moore**
Copywriter: **Joshua Prince**

Space Advertising

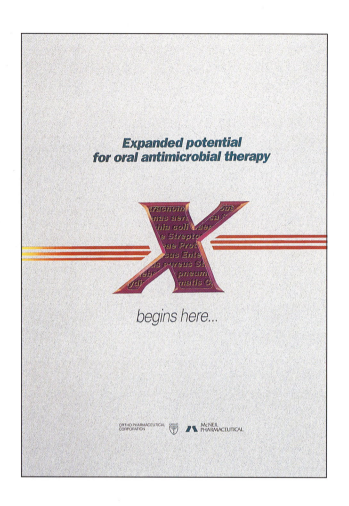

Product: **Floxin**
Title of Graphic: **Product Launch Advertising**
Ad Agency: **Botto, Roessner, Horne & Messinger**
Client: **Ortho Pharmaceutical Corp.**
Art Director: **Hector Padron**
Illustrator: **Doug Struthers, Lewis Calver**
Copywriter: **Susan Roessner, Cathy Popescu**

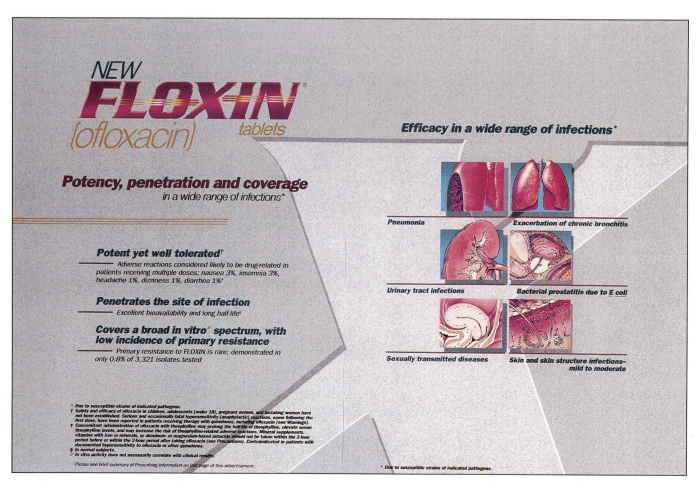

Space Advertising

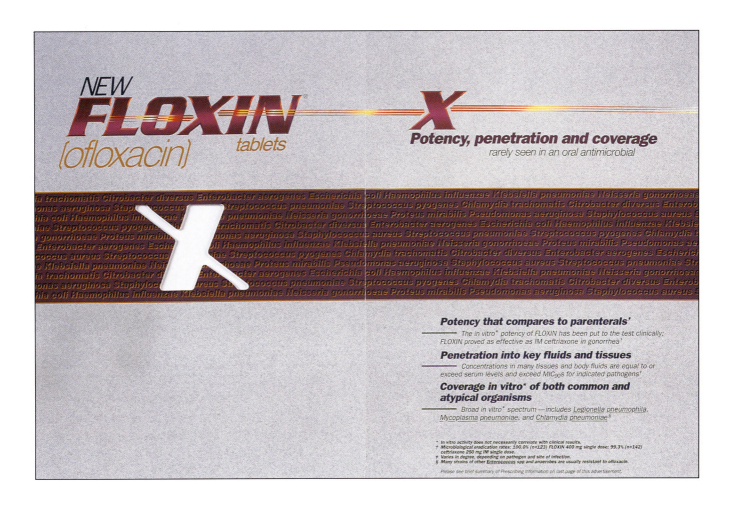

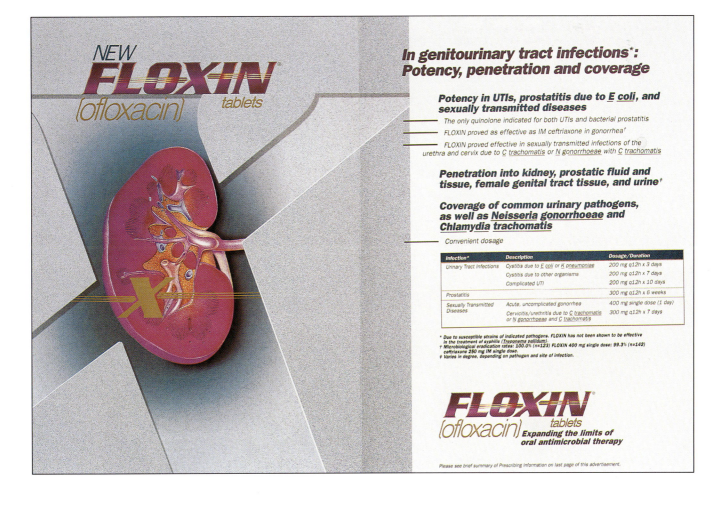

Space Advertising

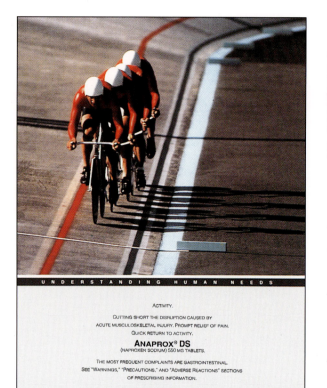

SILVER

Product: **Syntex Corporate**
Ad Agency: **Vicom/FCB**
Client: **Syntex**
Art Director: **Jerry Malone**
Photographer: **David Madison/David Buffington**
Copywriter: **Bob Finkel**

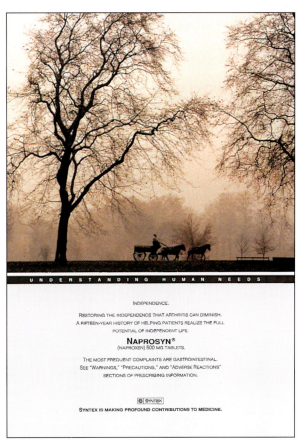

Space Advertising

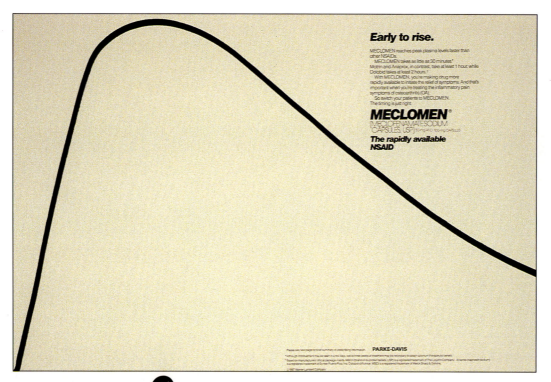

Product: **Meclomen**
Title of Graphic: **Early to Rise**
Ad Agency: **Sudler & Hennessey**
Client: **Parke-Davis, div. Warner Lambert Co.**
Art Director: **Rudi Sanchez/Steve Brothers**
Copywriter: **Steve Hamburg**

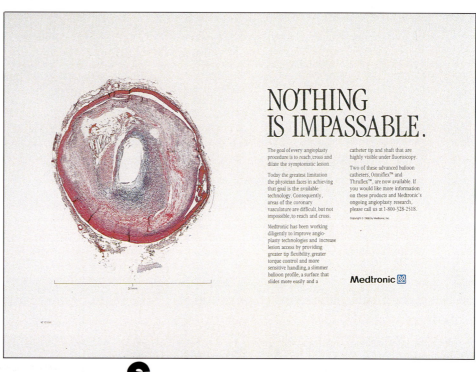

Product: **Omniflex and Thruflex Catheters**
Title of Graphic: **Nothing is Impassible**
Ad Agency: **Girgenti, Hughes, Butler & McDowell**
Client: **Medtronic**
Art Director: **Mark McDowell**
Copywriter: **Frank Hughes**

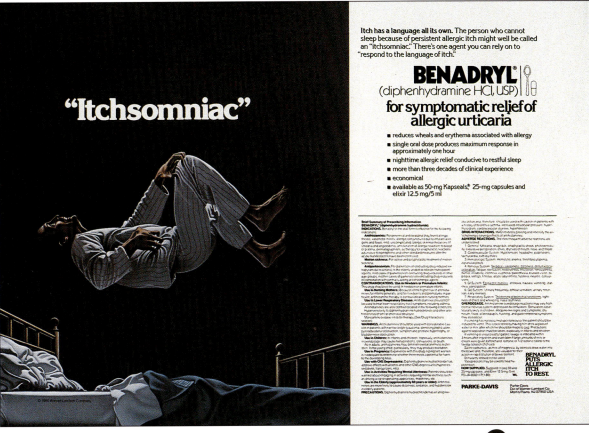

Product: **Benadryl**
Title of Graphic: **Itchsomniac**
Ad Agency: **Sudler & Hennessey**
Client: **Parke-Davis, div. Warner Lambert Co.**
Art Director: **Jim McFarland**
Copywriter: **Jack Speiller**

Product: **Kaon CL-10**
Title of Graphic: **One Billion Trips Down the G.I. Tract .... Without an Accident**
Ad Agency: **Lally, McFarland & Pantello, Inc.**
Client: **Adria Laboratories, Inc.**
Art Director: **Jim McFarland**
Copywriter: **John Lally**

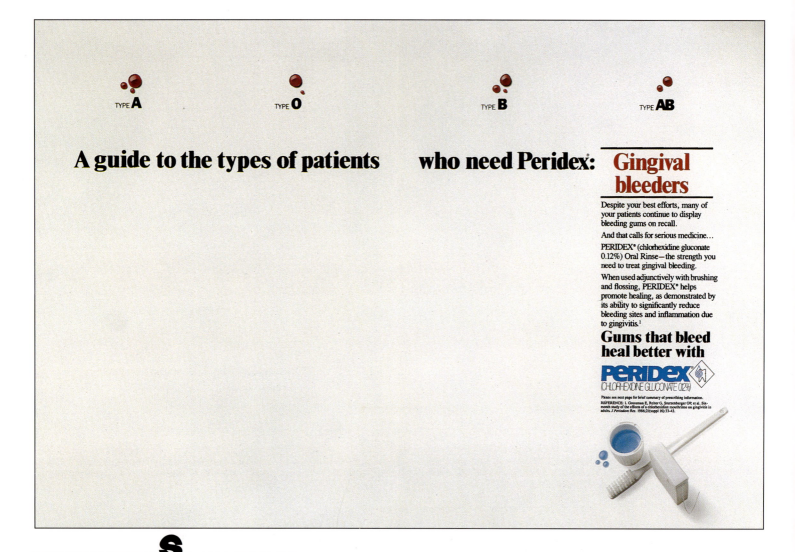

Product: **Peridex**
Title of Graphic: **Blood Types**
Ad Agency: **Lally, McFarland & Pantello, Inc.**
Client: **Proctor & Gamble, Inc.**
Art Director: **Julien Jarreau**
Photographers: **Roger Bester, Jim Greene**
Copywriter: **John Lally**

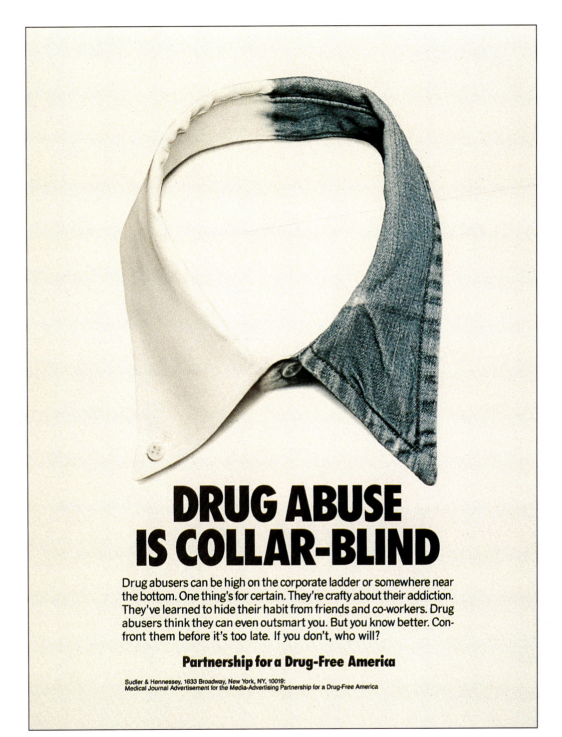

Product: **Public Service Ad**
Title of Graphic: **Drug Abuse is Collar-Blind**
Ad Agency: **Sudler & Hennessey**
Client: **Partnership for a Drug-Free America**
Art Director: **Dick Russinko**
Photographer: **John Olivo**
Copywriter: **Diane Cooney**

Space Advertising

Product: **EMLA**
Title of Graphic: **Maybe it's Time . . .**
Ad Agency: **SMW Advertising**
Client: **Astra Pharma Inc.**
Art Director: **David Sharpe/Michele Adams**
Illustrator: **Jerzy Kolacz**
Copywriter: **Judy Malone**

Maybe it's time for a whole new approach to local anesthetics.

Introducing EMLA.® The first topical anesthetic cream that can make needles virtually painless.

"This won't hurt a bit."
You may actually utter that phrase, but do you believe it? Your patients certainly don't.
Because the simple truth is, a needle can hurt. No matter how often a person gets one.
Now for the first time, you can effectively relieve the pain and fear your patients associate with a needle.[1,2]
With EMLA®, the first proven effective topical anesthetic cream to penetrate intact skin for virtually pain-free venipuncture.[1,2,3,4]
A unique mix of two well-known crystalline local anesthetics, lidocaine and prilocaine, EMLA® is formulated for patients of all ages, including children(not less than six months of age) who must undergo painful venipuncture.[5]
For intravenous injections, lumbar puncture, insertion of catheters, and any superficial procedure where intact skin is exposed to painful treatment, apply EMLA® as a premedication and cover with an occlusive dressing for at least one hour before treatment is initiated.[5]
EMLA® cream is a unique way to help your patients respond without fear when they see you.

Space Advertising

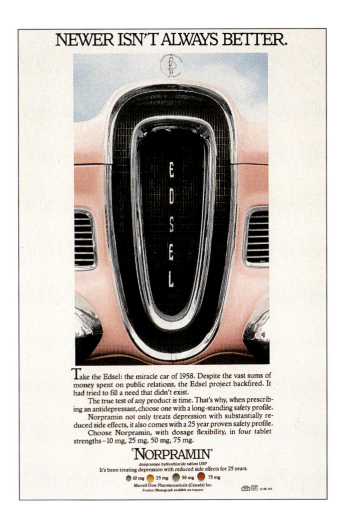

Product: **Norpramin**
Title of Graphic: **Newer isn't Always Better**
Ad Agency: **SMW Advertising**
Client: **Marion Merrell Dow Pharmaceuticals (Canada) Inc.**
Art Director: **Audrey Mayberry**
Photographer: **Miller Comstock**
Copywriter: **Karen Levenson**

Product: **Vivonex T.E.N.**
Title of Graphic: **AIDS Patients Can Starve on a Normal Diet**
Ad Agency: **Lally, McFarland & Pantello, Inc.**
Client: **Norwich Eaton Pharmaceuticals, Inc.**
Art Director: **Julien Jarreau**
Illustrator: **Alan Reingold**
Copywriter: **Cynthia Armstrong**

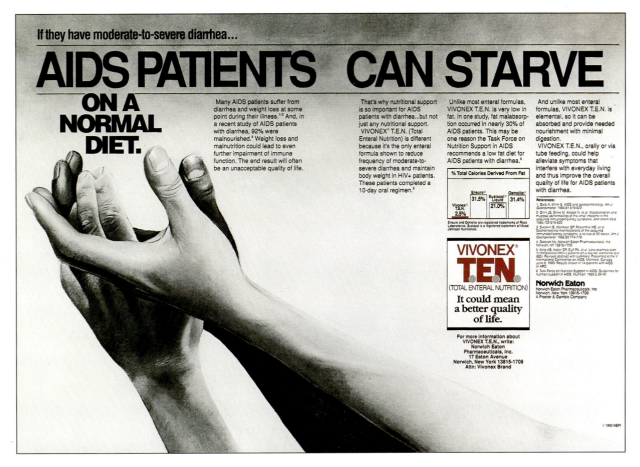

Product: **Disalcid**
Title of Graphic: **Unmatched**
Ad Agency: **Girgenti, Hughes, Butler & McDowell**
Client: **3M Pharmaceuticals**
Art Director: **Mark McDowell**
Illustrator: **Michael Schwab**
Copywriter: **Bob Ranieri**

Product: **Creon**
Title of Graphic: **Down to a Science**
Ad Agency: **Girgenti, Hughes, Butler & McDowell**
Client: **Solvay**
Art Director: **Mark McDowell**
Illustrator: **Jeff Holewski**
Copywriter: **Frank Hughes**

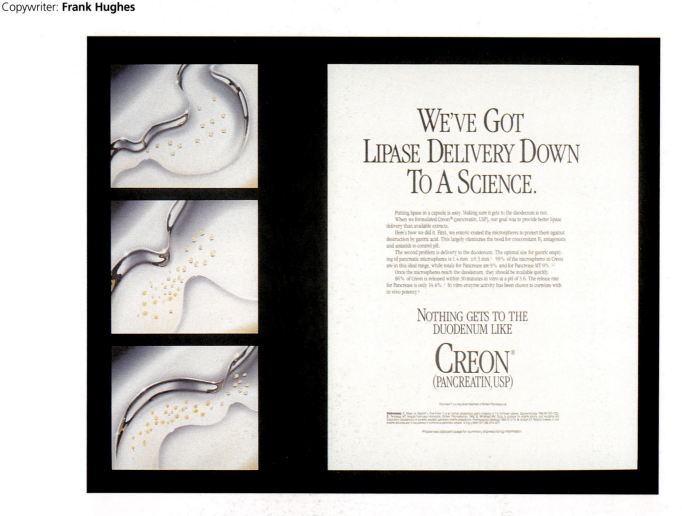

Space Advertising

Product: **Imovane**
Title of Graphic: **New Imovane Covers the Night Without Clouding The Day**
Ad Agency: **Lally, McFarland & Pantello (Canada) Ltd.**
Client: **Rhone-Poulenc Rorer (Canada)**
Art Director: **Julien Jarreau/Paul Gioni**
Illustrator: **John Martin**
Copywriter: **Steve West**

Product: **Denquel**
Title of Graphic: **Do the Foods Your Patients Love Sometimes Bite Back?**
Ad Agency: **Lally, McFarland & Pantello, Inc.**
Client: **Procter & Gamble**
Art Director: **Audrey Sanchez**
Illustrator: **Matthew Holmes**
Copywriter: **Susan Greenhut**

Space Advertising

Product: **Elite**
Title of Graphic: **Heart's Desire**
Ad Agency: **Girgenti, Hughes, Butler & McDowell**
Client: **Medtronic**
Art Director: **Mark McDowell**
Photographer: **Marc Cohen**
Copywriter: **Frank Hughes**

Product: **Bromfed**
Title of Graphic: **Beastly**
Ad Agency: **Girgenti, Hughes, Butler & McDowell**
Client: **Muro Pharmaceuticals**
Art Director: **Scott Frank**
Illustrator: **Alexandra Ranieri**
Photographer: **John Manno**
Copywriter: **Bob Ranieri**

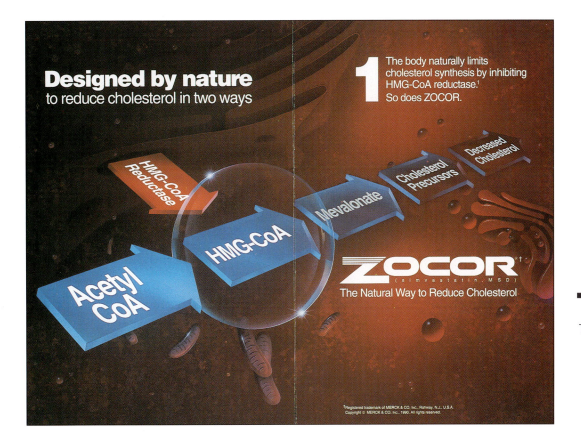
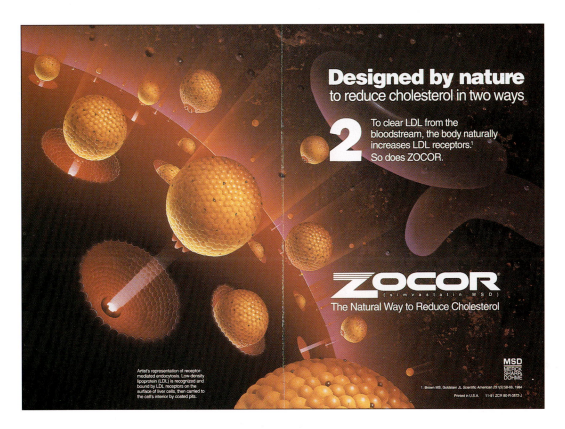

Product: **Zocor**
Title of Graphic: **Mechanism of Action Ad Campaign**
Design Firm: **The Hal Lewis Group**
Client: **Merck Sharp & Dohme International**
Art Director: **David Winigrad**
Illustrator: **Keith Kasnot**
Copywriter: **Alan Rubin**

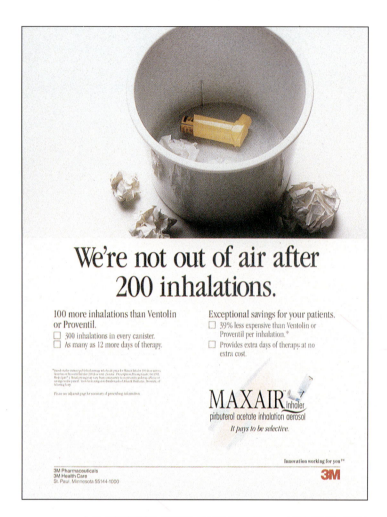

Product: **Maxair**
Title of Graphic: **Out of Air**
Ad Agency: **Girgenti, Hughes, Butler & McDowell**
Client: **3M Pharmaceuticals**
Art Director: **Scott Frank**
Photographer: **John Manno**
Copywriter: **Bob Ranieri**

Product: **Vivonex T.E.N.**
Title of Graphic: **Dinner After the Theatre**
Ad Agency: **Lally, McFarland & Pantello, Inc.**
Client: **Norwich Eaton Pharmaceuticals, Inc.**
Art Director: **Rudy Sanchez**
Photographer: **Bob Walsh**
Copywriter: **Steve West**

Space Advertising

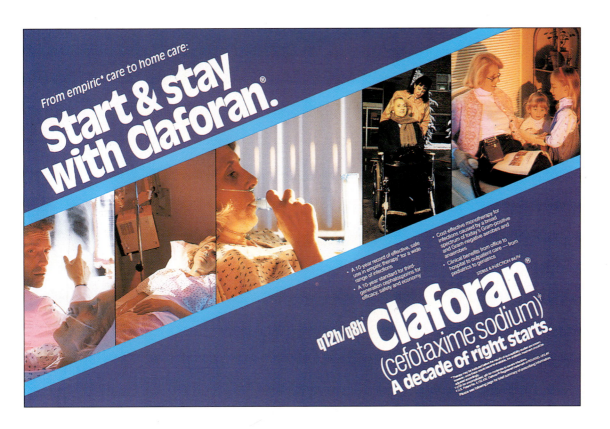

Product: **Claforan (cefotaxime sodium)**
Title of Graphic: **Start & Stay with Claforan**
Ad Agency: **Wm. Douglas McAdams, Inc.**
Client: **Hoechst-Rousell Pharmaceuticals**
Art Director: **Patrick Creaven/ Dave Kingham**
Photographer: **Shig Ikeda**
Copywriter: **Gwenne Frieman**

Product: **M.S. Contin (morphine sulfate controlled-release)**
Title of Graphic: **The Spectre of Cancer Pain. Keep it at Bay.**
Ad Agency: **Wm. Douglas McAdams, Inc.**
Client: **Purdue Frederick Company**
Art Director: **Patrick Creaven/ Diane Lynch**
Photographer: **Howard Berman**
Copywriter: **Gwenne Frieman/ Jules Korzenowski**

Product: **Cardizem SR**
Title of Graphic: **Down Safe**
Ad Agency: **RWR Advertising, Inc.**
Client: **Marion Merrell Dow**
Art Director: **Rick Reddy**
Photographer: **Brett Froomer**
Copywriter: **Carole Post/Barbara Huber**

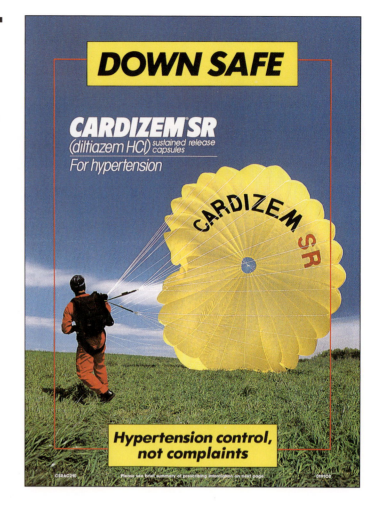

Product: **Buspar**
Title of Graphic: **Once Everyone Believed . . .**
Ad Agency: **SMW Advertising**
Client: **Bristol-Myers Squibb**
Art Director: **Rich Buceta**
Photographer: **Bettman Newsphotos**
Copywriter: **Gary Lennox**

Space Advertising

Product: **Clozaril (clozapine)**
Title of Graphic: **Four-Page Ad Insert**
Ad Agency: **M.E.D. Communications**
Client: **Sandoz Pharmaceuticals**
Art Director: **Jim Crispo**
Photographer: **Neil Molinaro**
Copywriter: **Jack Speiller/Mike Brune**
Model Maker: **Ron Terrill**

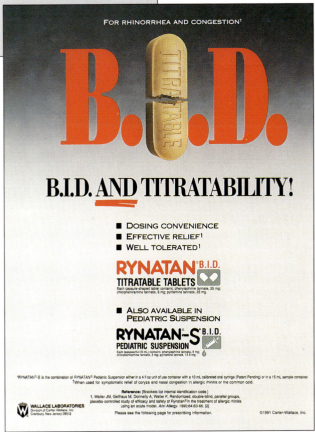

Product: **Rynatan Tablets**
Title of Graphic: **B.I.D.**
Ad Agency: **RWR Advertising, Inc.**
Client: **Wallace Labs**
Art Director: **George Armstrong**
Illustrator: **Tartaro Slavin, Inc.**
Copywriter: **Janice McGuirl**

Space Advertising

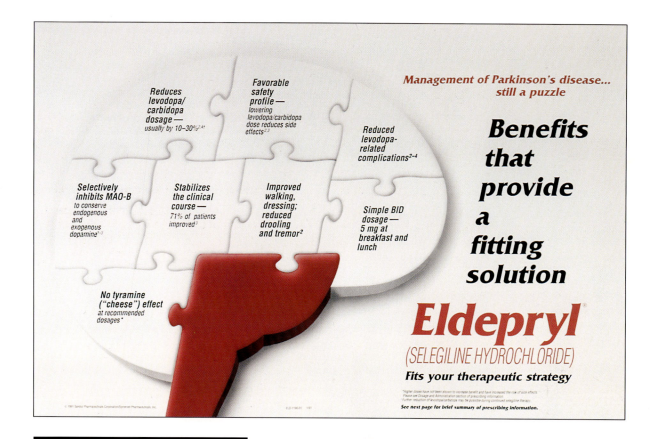

Product: **Eldepryl**
Title of Graphic: **Eldepryl Journal Ad**
Ad Agency: **M.E.D. Communications**
Client: **Sandoz Pharmaceuticals**
Art Director: **Frank Kacmarsky**
Illustrator: **Steve Heimann**
Copywriter: **Nancy Sokasits**

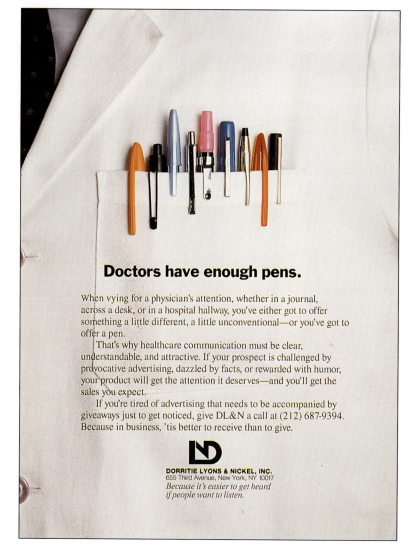

Title of Graphic: **Doctors Have Enough Pens**
Ad Agency: **Dorritie Lyons & Nickel**
Art Director: **Mike Lyons**
Photographer: **Shig Ikeda**
Copywriter: **Scott Robbins**

Space Advertising

41

Product: **Kodak Ektachem Analyzers**
Title of Graphic: **Bottom Line: Satisfaction Guaranteed**
Ad Agency: **J. Walter Thompson Healthcare**
Client: **Eastman Kodak**
Art Director: **Bill Alderisio**

Product: **Ektachem 700XR Analyzer**
Title of Graphic: **Alone at the Top**
Ad Agency: **J. Walter Thompson Healthcare**
Client: **Eastman Kodak Clinical**
Art Director: **Bill Alderisio**
Photographer: **Steve Kelly/Kodak Premier System**

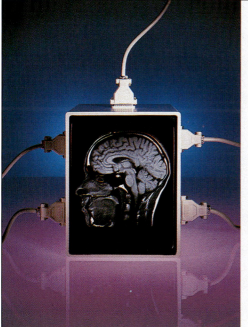

Product: **Kodak Ektascan Laser Printer**
Title of Graphic: **Smart, Well-Connected**
Ad Agency: **J. Walter Thompson Healthcare**
Client: **Eastman Kodak Health Sciences**
Art Director: **Bill Alderisio**
Photographer: **Shig Ikeda**

Space Advertising

Product: **Benadryl**
Title of Graphic: **Keep Itch Patients From Climbing the Walls . . .**
Ad Agency: **Sudler & Hennessey**
Client: **Parke-Davis, Consumer Health Products Group**
Art Director: **Meg Levine**
Photographer: **Steve Bronstein**
Copywriter: **Sandra Holtzman**
Model Maker: **Mark Budrow**

Product: **Fortaz (ceftazidime) and Zinacef (cefuroxime sodium)**
Title of Graphic: **We're Not Just a Name**
Ad Agency: **Kallir, Philips, Ross, Inc.**
Client: **Glaxo Pharmaceuticals, Inc.**
Art Director: **James Burton**
Photographer: **Bill White**
Copywriter: **Joanne H. Dalton**

Space Advertising

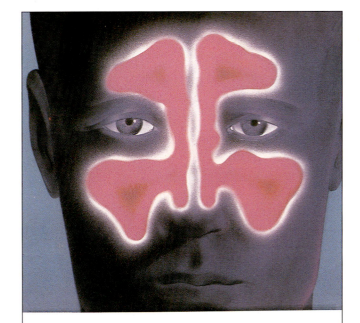

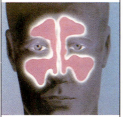

Product: **Advil Cold & Sinus**
Title of Graphic: **For Pain or Fever as Well as Congestion**
Ad Agency: **Sudler & Hennessey**
Client: **Whitehall Laboratories**
Art Director: **Joe Chierchio**
Illustrator: **Carol Gillot**
Copywriter: **Joanne Peppard**

Product: **Zaroxolyn**
Title of Graphic: **Special Effects**
Ad Agency: **Sandler Communications**
Client: **Fisons Pharmaceuticals**
Art Director: **Adam Cohen**
Illustrator: **Craig Zuckerman — R. Greenburg Associates**
Copywriter: **Lydia Greene**

43

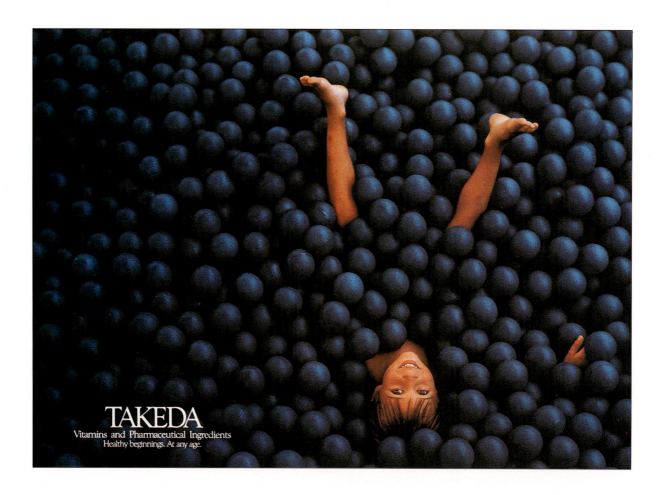

Product: **Vitamins and Pharmaceutical Ingredients**
Title of Graphic: **Blue Boy**
Ad Agency: **Koehler Iversen, Inc.**
Client: **Takeda USA, Inc.**
Art Director: **Leon Kislowski**
Photographer: **Peter Poulides**
Copywriter: **W. Peter Koehler**

Product: **Vitamins and Pharmaceutical Ingredients**
Title of Graphic: **Asparagus**
Ad Agency: **Koehler Iversen, Inc.**
Client: **Takeda USA, Inc.**
Art Director: **Leon Kislowski**
Photographer: **Craig Stewart**
Copywriter: **W. Peter Koehler**

Space Advertising

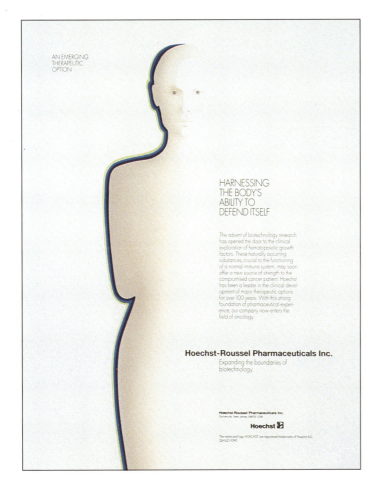

Product: **Sandimmune**
Title of Graphic: **She Practices With All Her Heart**
Ad Agency: **Integrated Communications Corp.**
Client: **Sandoz Pharmaceuticals**
Art Director: **Lin Kossak**
Photographer: **John Cooper**
Copywriter: **Charles DeMarco**

Product: **Prokine**
Ad Agency: **Thomas G. Ferguson Associates, Inc.**
Client: **Hoechst-Roussel Pharmaceuticals**
Art Director: **Barbara McCullough**
Illustrator: **Jeff Holewski**
Copywriter: **Diane Iler-Smith**

Product: **Zinkorotat**
Title of Graphic: **The Bodyguard, The Skin's Friend, The Immunity Fortifier, The Healer**
Ad Agency: **Sudler & Hennessey Frankfurt**
Client: **Ursapharm Arzneimittel GmbH**
Art Director: **Birgit Scherer**
Creative Director: **Hans Odenbach**
Photographer: **Klaus Peter Nordmann**
Copywriter: **Mascha Linke**

Natural Latex Rubber Gloves Could Be The Root Of Your Skin Problems.

If you suffer from contact urticaria, allergic contact dermatitis, or local pruritus, your problems may stem from the fact that most disposable gloves are made from natural latex rubber.

In making ordinary surgical gloves, raw latex is harvested from rubber trees growing in tropical jungles, and combined with thiuram accelerators, sulfur donors, antioxidants, surfactants and various acids.

Often, the chemicals used in the manufacture of latex surgical gloves are responsible for these irritating skin problems.[1] Contaminants such as tree bark, molds, fungi, lichen, and other insoluble proteins are frequently present in natural latex, and further compound the problem.

Now there's an alternative – Tactylon™ Non-latex Hypoallergenic Surgical Gloves.

Unlike ordinary hypoallergenic gloves that are made from latex, our new gloves are made from a non-latex synthetic polymer. So, they contain none of the chemicals, organic contaminants or impurities associated with natural latex rubber gloves.

New Tactylon gloves offer enhanced reliability and longer shelf life because they will not weaken over time the way natural latex does when exposed to heat, ozone and extended storage. But, the true test of these remarkable new surgical gloves is in your hands. Or rather, on your hands. That's why we'll send you a FREE pair, and our informative pamphlet, when you call toll-free 1-800-TACTYLON (1-800-822-8956) today.

You'll find that comfort and reliability go hand in hand.

NEW
TACTYLON™
NON-LATEX HYPOALLERGENIC SURGICAL GLOVES

SMARTPRACTICE
3400 East McDowell
Phoenix, AZ 85008-3846
1-800-TACTYLON
1-800-822-8956

1. Maso MJ, Goldberg DJ: Contact dermatoses from disposable glove use: A review. *J Am Acad Dermatol* 1990;23:733-737. ©1991 SmartPractice

---

Product: **Tactylon**
Title of Graphic: **Jungle Ad**
Ad Agency: **Baxter, Gurian and Mazzei, Inc.**
Client: **Smart Practice**
Art Director: **Alan Ichiriu**
Illustrator: **Robert Giusti**
Copywriter: **Steve Sperber**

Space Advertising

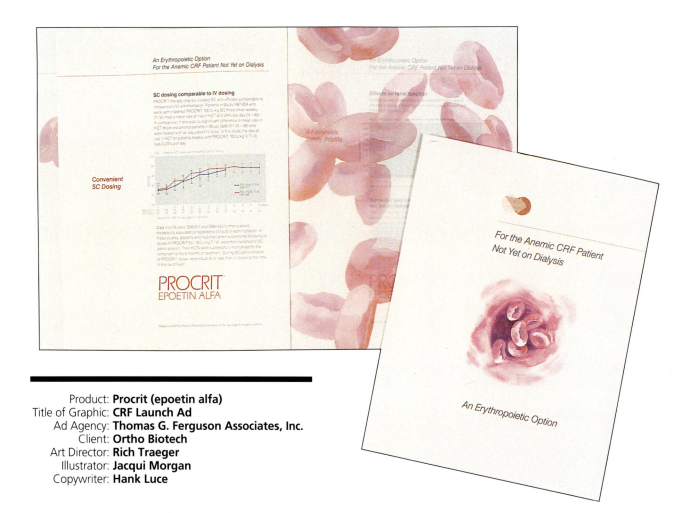

Product: **Procrit (epoetin alfa)**
Title of Graphic: **CRF Launch Ad**
Ad Agency: **Thomas G. Ferguson Associates, Inc.**
Client: **Ortho Biotech**
Art Director: **Rich Traeger**
Illustrator: **Jacqui Morgan**
Copywriter: **Hank Luce**

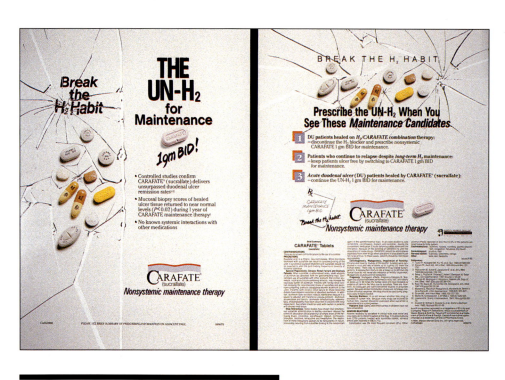

Product: **Carafate**
Title of Graphic: **Break the H_2 Habit Ad**
Ad Agency: **McCann Healthcare Advertising**
Client: **Marion Merrell Dow**
Art Director: **Geoff Melick**
Photographer: **Richard Hertzberg**
Copywriter: **Scott Hansen**

Space Advertising

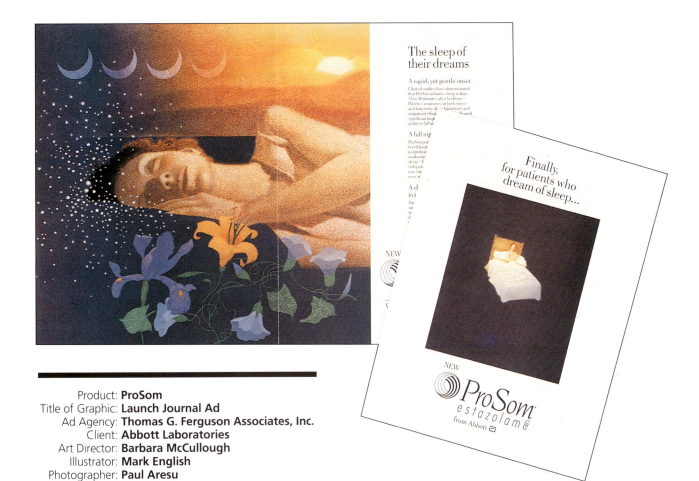

Product: **ProSom**
Title of Graphic: **Launch Journal Ad**
Ad Agency: **Thomas G. Ferguson Associates, Inc.**
Client: **Abbott Laboratories**
Art Director: **Barbara McCullough**
Illustrator: **Mark English**
Photographer: **Paul Aresu**
Copywriter: **Tom Spellman**

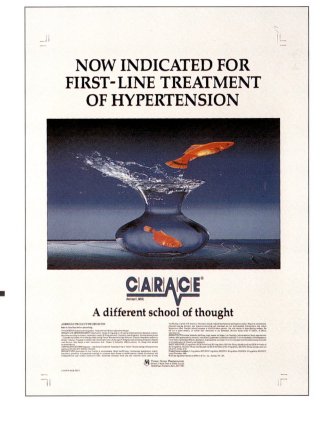

Product: **Carace**
Title of Graphic: **First-Line Indication Ad**
Ad Agency: **Medicus Communications Ltd.**
Client: **MSD**
Art Director: **Shirley Hart**
Photographer: **Howard Kingsnorth**
Copywriter: **Clayton Love**

Space Advertising

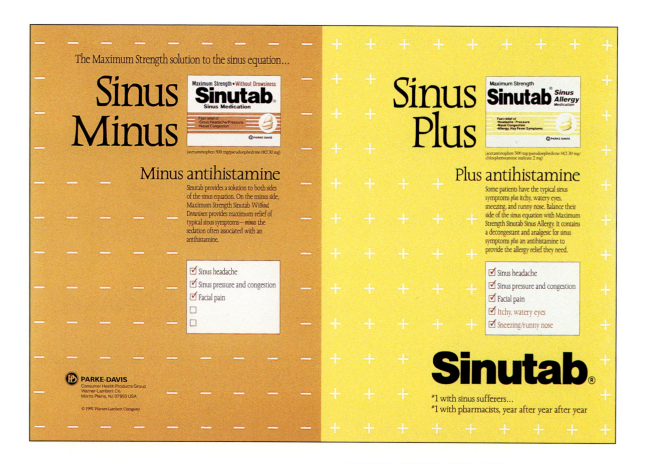

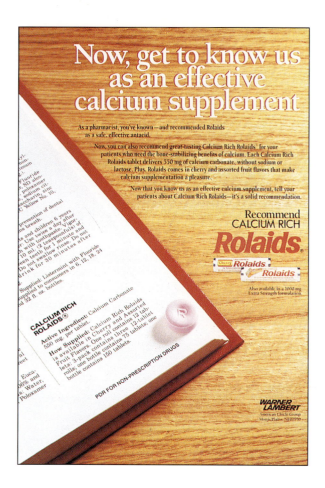

Product: **Sinutab**
Title of Graphic: **Sinus Minus . . . Sinus Plus**
Ad Agency: **Thomas G. Ferguson Associates, Inc.**
Client: **Warner Lambert**
Art Director: **Sue Cunningham/Irene Bonner**
Illustrator: **Steve Heimann**
Copywriter: **Marcia Blaustein**

Product: **Rolaids**
Title of Graphic: **Get to Know Us**
Ad Agency: **Thomas G. Ferguson Associates, Inc.**
Client: **Warner-Lambert**
Art Director: **Mark J. Rusinack**
Photographer: **Jeff Morgan**
Copywriter: **Hank Luce**

Space Advertising

Product: **Anaprox DS**
Title of Graphic: **Reclining Lady**
Ad Agency: **Baxter, Gurian and Mazzei, Inc.**
Client: **Syntex**
Art Director: **Alan Ichiriu**
Photographer: **Glen Wexler**
Copywriter: **Bill Melhourn**

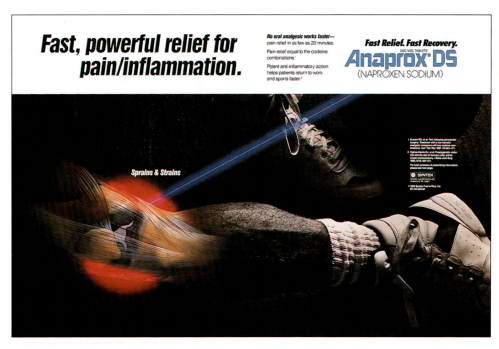

Product: **Anaprox DS**
Title of Graphic: **Knee**
Ad Agency: **Baxter, Gurian and Mazzei, Inc.**
Client: **Syntex**
Art Director: **Alan Ichiriu**
Photographer: **Glen Wexler**
Copywriter: **Bill Melhourn**

Space Advertising

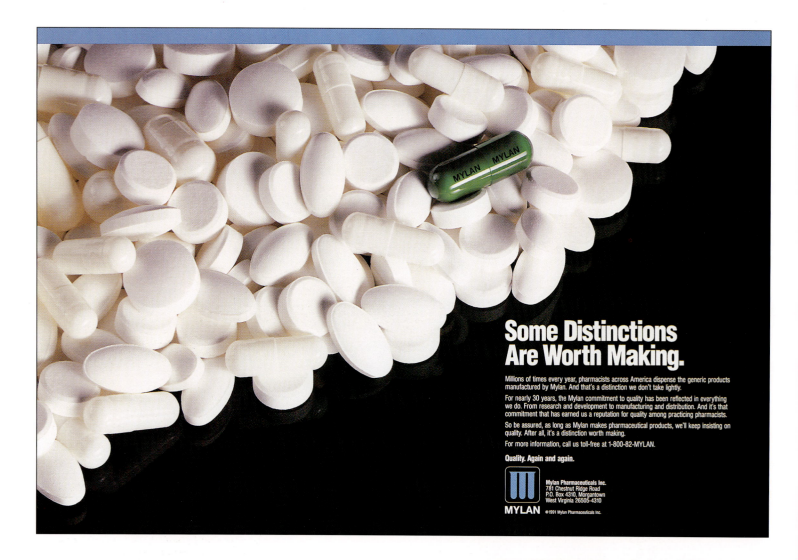

Title of Graphic: **Some Distinctions are Worth Making**
Ad Agency: **Rienzi & Rienzi Communications, Inc.**
Client: **Mylan Pharmaceuticals Inc.**
Art Director: **Mary Gayle Scheper**
Photographer: **Frank Aiello**
Copywriter: **James Donal Sheridan**

Space Advertising

Product: **Aquaphor Faster Healing Ointments**
Title of Graphic: **Aquaphor Gun Slingers**
Ad Agency: **Hall Decker McKibbin, Inc.**
Client: **Beiersdorf, Inc.**
Art Director: **Doreen Sabatino**
Photographer: **John Campos**
Copywriter: **Wendy Friedman**

Product: **Fybogel Orange**
Title of Graphic: **Clockwork Orange**
Ad Agency: **Medicus Communications Ltd.**
Client: **Reckitt & Colman**
Art Director: **Shirley Hart/Shelanne Dickie**
Photographer: **Jay Myrdal**
Copywriter: **Jacqui Hogan**

Product: **Braun Oral-B Plaque Remover**
Title of Graphic: **Removes Even the Most Stubborn Excuse**
Ad Agency: **Rainoldi Kerzner Radcliffe**
Client: **Braun, Inc./Oral-B Laboratories**
Art Director: **Paschal Sabatella**
Photographer: **Paul Franz-Moore**
Copywriter: **Jeremiah Treacy**

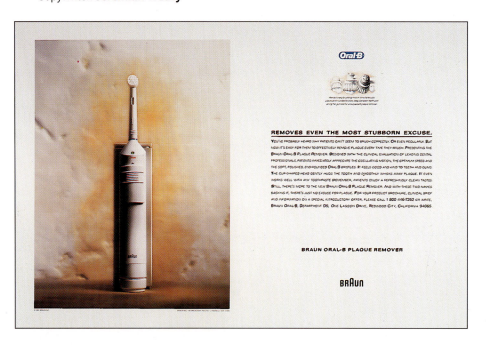

Product: **Oral-B Minute-Gel APF Topical Flouride;
Oral-B Centrays and Centwins Applicator Trays**
Title of Graphic: **Up to the Minute Program**
Ad Agency: **Rainoldi Kerzner Radcliffe**
Client: **Oral-B Laboratories**
Art Director: **Paschal Sabatella**
Photographer: **Paul Franz-Moore**
Copywriter: **Jeremiah Treacy**

Space Advertising

THIS IS HISTORY

AND HISTORY IS ABOUT TO REPEAT ITSELF

The ONE TOUCH® meter made history. It revolutionized simple, accurate blood glucose monitoring with the first non-wipe technology. In fact, for over three years it's been the non-wipe meter selected by more hospitals. Now, history advances to the future—with the ONE TOUCH II meter. It features the same hospital-proven, patient-preferred ONE TOUCH technology. Accuracy. Simplicity. Even the same test strips.

INTRODUCING THE NEW ONE TOUCH® II

And compared to other meters, clinical studies prove the new ONE TOUCH II meter is more accurate where it really counts—right in the hands of your patients.* So take a look at the ONE TOUCH II meter. To see our accuracy, we'll show you the clinical studies. To see our simplicity, we'll show you the meter. Please call your LifeScan Professional Representative, or 1 800 227-8862. And bring history up to date.

BLOOD GLUCOSE METER FROM LIFESCAN

*Portable, convenient and as you can see, easy on the eye.
We're showing it actual size.

Product: **One Touch II Blood Glucose Monitor**
Title of Graphic: **This is History**
Ad Agency: **Rainoldi Kerzner Radcliffe**
Client: **LifeScan Inc.**
Art Director: **Mark Trippetti**
Photographer: **Paul Franz-Moore**
Copywriter: **Hal Bruster/Patricia Malone**

HISTORY BRINGS YOU WITHIN ONE TOUCH OF THE FUTURE

Press power. Insert a test strip.

And place a drop of blood on it. There's no wiping, no timing or blotting.

Just 45 seconds and accurate results are confidently in hand.

Our Commitment To You. Our goal is to provide you with quality healthcare products and dedicated customer service. To make sure your patients are satisfied, we offer a No-Risk, Money-Back Guarantee and will refund their purchase within 30 days. Should you have any questions about this or any other LifeScan product, please call 1 800 227-8862. Thank you.

Accuracy Made Simple.
LIFESCAN

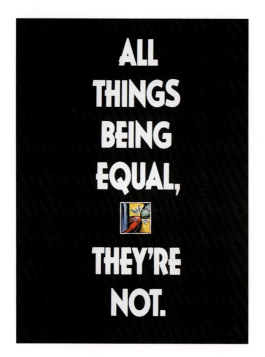
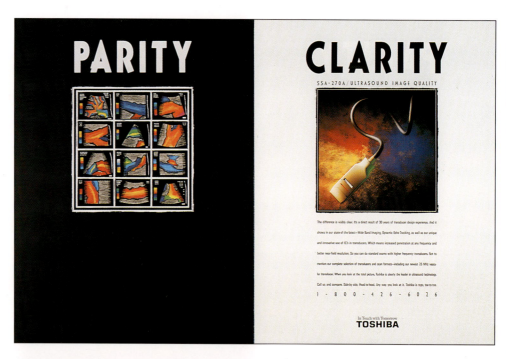
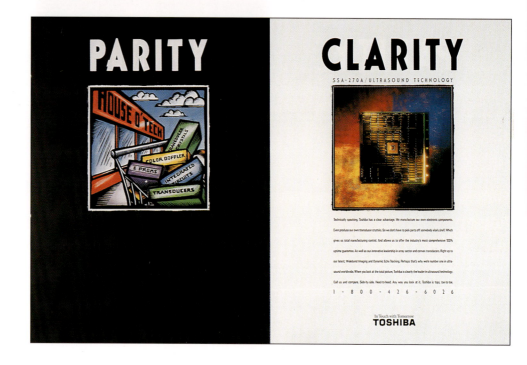

Product: **Toshiba SSH-140A Ultrasound System**
Title of Graphic: **All Things Being Equal**
Ad Agency: **Rainoldi Kerzner Radcliffe**
Client: **Toshiba America Medical Systems**
Art Director: **Mark Trippetti**
Illustrator: **Judd Guitteau**
Photographer: **Paul Franz-Moore**
Copywriter: **Hal Bruster**

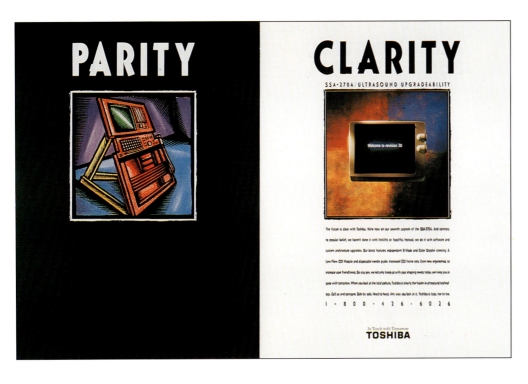
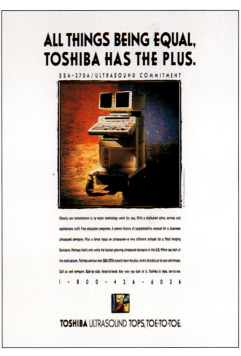

Product: **Salazopyrin EN**
Title of Graphic: **Arthritic Dressing**
Ad Agency: **Plato Healthcare Promotions**
Client: **Keatings**
Art Director: **Linda Rademan**
Photographer: **Ian Difford**
Copywriter: **Peter Fraser**

Product: **Halcion**
Title of Graphic: **Good Nights**
Ad Agency: **Plato Healthcare Promotions**
Client: **Upjohn**
Art Director: **Ian Dobell**
Photographer: **Michael Ehrman**
Copywriter: **Linda Ackermann**

Space Advertising

Product: **Pondocillin**
Title of Graphic: **Is a Penicillin . . .**
Ad Agency: **Plato Healthcare Promotions**
Client: **Leo Medical**
Art Director: **Ian Dobell**
Illustrator: **Bernie De Haas**
Copywriter: **Linda Ackermann**

Product: **Magnevist**
Title of Graphic: **Vague Symptoms**
Ad Agency: **Sudler & Hennessey**
Client: **Berlex Laboratories, Inc.**
Art Director: **Dick Russinko**
Copywriter: **Diane Cooney/Joe Garamella**

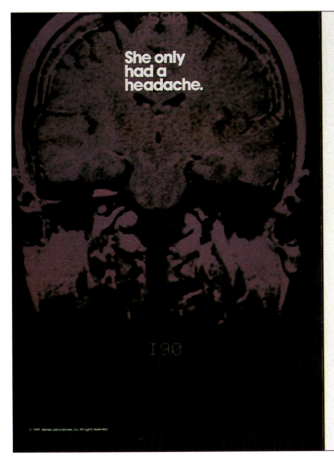

Space Advertising

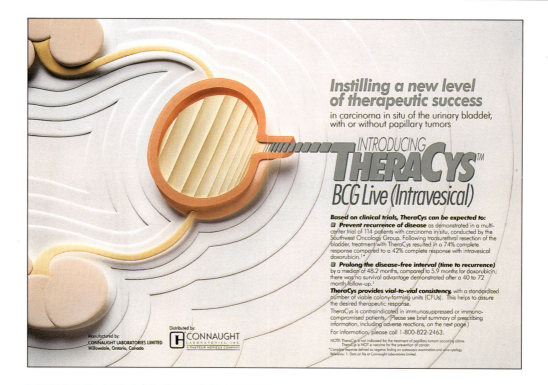

Product: **TheraCys**
Title of Graphic: **Paper Sculpture of Urinary Bladder**
Ad Agency: **Barnum & Souza, Inc.**
Client: **Connaught Laboratories, Inc.**
Art Director: **Fran Davies**
Copywriter: **Marjorie Vincent/Carla Olinger**
Structural Design: **Michael Raden Studios**

Product: **Theo-Dur**
Title of Graphic: **It Takes Balls . . .**
Ad Agency: **Plato Healthcare Promotions**
Client: **Rio Ethicals**
Art Director: **Ian Dobell**
Photographer: **Mike Leisegang**
Copywriter: **Linda Ackermann**

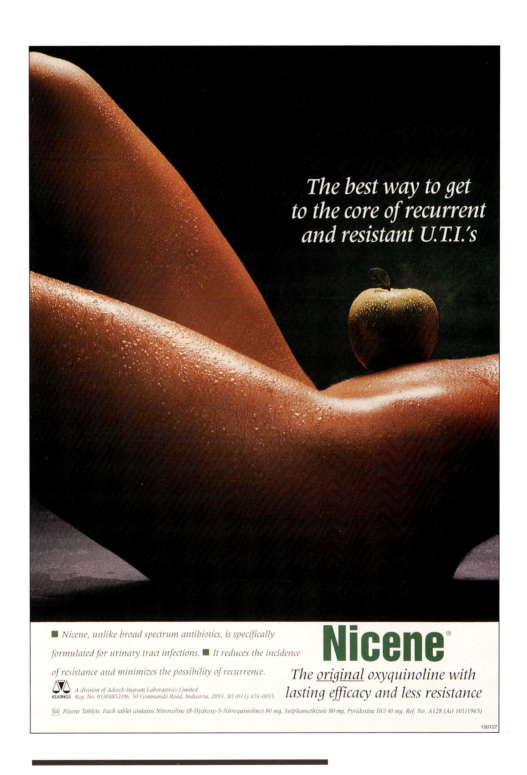

Product: **Nicene**
Title of Graphic: **The Best Way . . .**
Ad Agency: **Plato Healthcare Promotions**
Client: **Keatings Pharmaceuticals**
Art Director: **Ian Dobell**
Photographer: **Louis Fouche**
Copywriter: **Linda Ackermann**

Space Advertising

Product: **Corporate Promotion**
Title of Graphic: **Baby Blowing Bubbles**
Ad Agency: **Barnum & Souza, Inc.**
Client: **Connaught Laboratories, Inc.**
Art Director: **Fran Davies**
Photographer: **David Siegel**
Copywriter: **Marjorie Vincent**

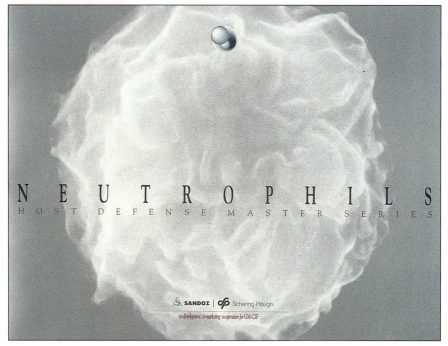

Product: **Leucomax**
Title of Graphic: **Neutrophils — Host Defense Master Series #1**
Ad Agency: **Integrated Communications Corp.**
Client: **Sandoz Pharmaceuticals/Schering-Plough**
Art Director: **John Bernegger**
Illustrator: **Scott Barrows**
Copywriter: **Don Tessier**

Space Advertising

Product: **Barrier Packs — Fluid Collection Systems**
Title of Graphic: **We've Been Helping You Collect Fluid for Years**
Ad Agency: **Pierce-Davis & Associates**
Client: **Johnson & Johnson Medical, Inc.**
Art Director: **Bill Galyean**
Photographer: **Steve Hamblin**
Copywriter: **Margie Bowles**

Product: **Oil of Olay**
Title of Graphic: **Everyday is Sun-Day**
Ad Agency: **Gross Townsend Frank Hoffman**
Client: **Proctor & Gamble**
Art Director: **Miles West/Jim Lolis**
Photographer: **Stock**
Copywriter: **Banning Repplier**

Product: **Nuprin**
Title of Graphic: **Aching for Nuprin**
Ad Agency: **Gross Townsend Frank Hoffman**
Client: **Bristol-Myers**
Art Director: **Orin Kimball**
Photographer: **Martin Mistretta**
Copywriter: **Dana Delibovi**

Space Advertising

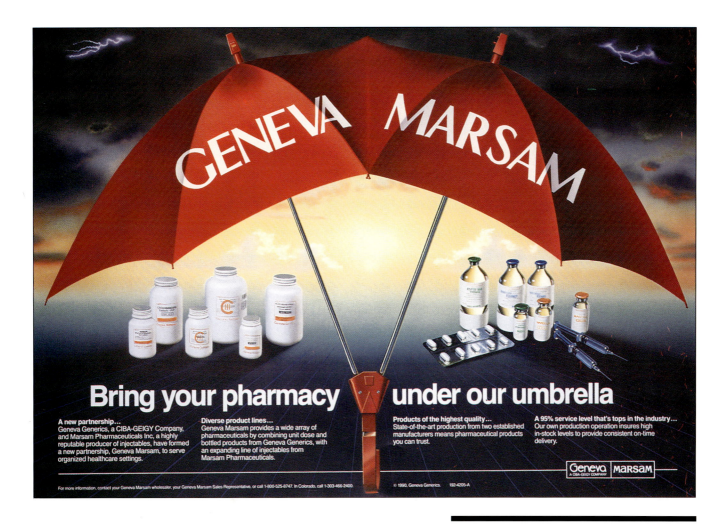

Title of Graphic: **Geneva Marsam Intro Ad**
Ad Agency: **C & G Advertising Agency, Inc.**
Client: **Geneva Marsam**
Art Director: **Ron Vareltzis**
Illustrator: **Steve Hieman**
Copywriter: **John Lewis**
Artist: **Steve Martin**

Product: **Pulmicort**
Title of Graphic: **Everyday Simplicity**
Ad Agency: **Sudler & Hennessey**
Client: **Astra Pharmaceuticals UK**
Art Director: **Jack Harris**
Illustrator: **Frank Langford**
Copywriter: **Paul Paech**

Space Advertising

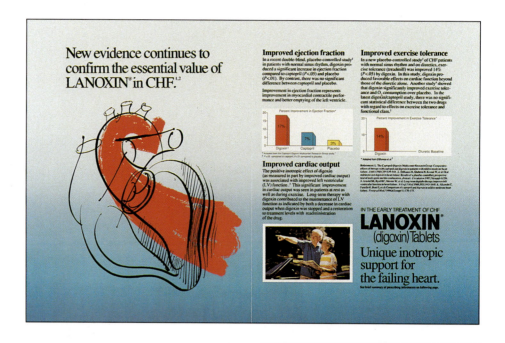

Product: **Lopid**
Title of Graphic: **Road Signs**
Ad Agency: **Sudler & Hennessey**
Client: **Parke Davis Pty Ltd.**
Art Director: **Martin Kane**
Photographer: **Phil Haley**
Copywriter: **Robert Lallamant**

Product: **Lanoxin**
Title of Graphic: **Japanese Heart**
Ad Agency: **Lavey/Wolff/Swift**
Client: **Burroughs Wellcome Co.**
Art Director: **Kenneth Lavey**
Illustrator: **Kenneth Lavey**
Copywriter: **Michael Metelenis**

Space Advertising

Product: **Nitradisc**
Title of Graphic: **Frustrating**
Ad Agency: **Sudler & Hennessey**
Client: **Searle Laboratories**
Art Director: **Chris Bull**
Photographer: **John Porter**
Copywriter: **Diane Ohye**

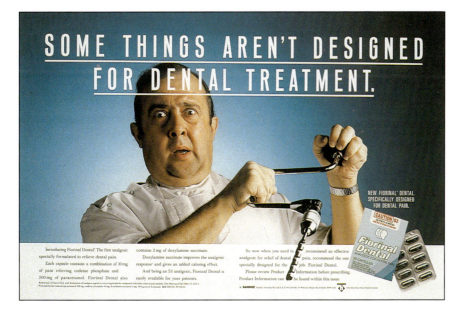

Product: **Fiorinal Dental**
Title of Graphic: **Drill**
Ad Agency: **Sudler & Hennessey**
Client: **Sandoz Australia**
Art Director: **Chris Bull**
Photographer: **John Porter**
Copywriter: **Tim Phillp**

Product: **Oral-B Toothbrushes**
Title of Graphic: **Excellence, Always**
Ad Agency: **Rainoldi Kerzner Radcliffe**
Client: **Oral-B Laboratories**
Art Director: **Paschal Sabatella**
Photographer: **Ernie Friedlander**
Copywriter: **Jeremiah Treacy**

Space Advertising

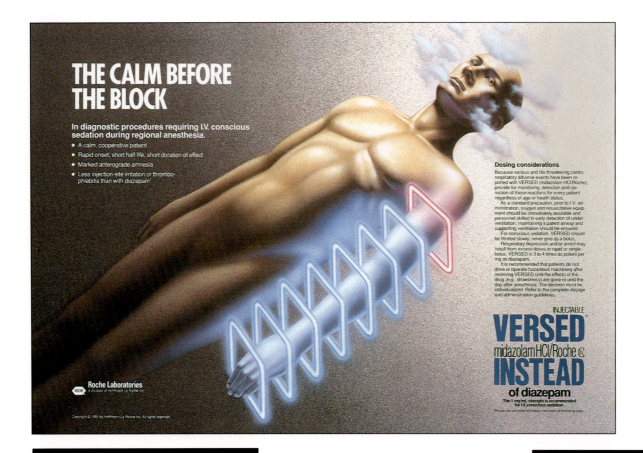

Product: **Versed**
Title of Graphic: **The Calm Before the Block**
Ad Agency: **William Douglas McAdams**
Client: **Roche Laboratories**
Art Director: **Carl Opalek/John Male**
Illustrator: **Jerry Lofaro**
Copywriter: **John Avery**

Product: **Versed**
Title of Graphic: **Added Stability . . .**
Ad Agency: **William Douglas McAdams**
Client: **Roche Laboratories**
Art Director: **Carl Opalek**
Illustrator: **Randee Ladden**
Photographer: **Paul Frankian**
Copywriter: **John Avery**

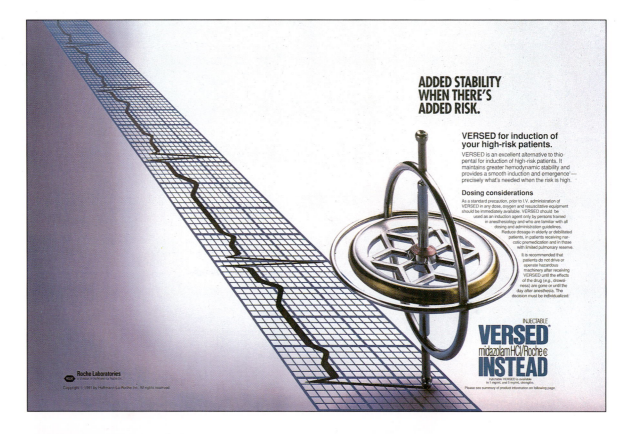

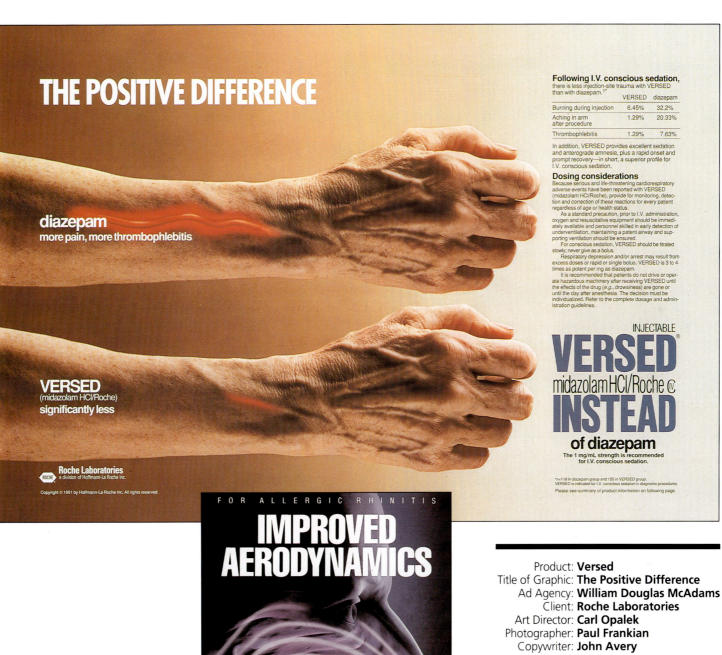

Product: **Versed**
Title of Graphic: **The Positive Difference**
Ad Agency: **William Douglas McAdams**
Client: **Roche Laboratories**
Art Director: **Carl Opalek**
Photographer: **Paul Frankian**
Copywriter: **John Avery**

Product: **Nasalide**
Title of Graphic: **Improved Aerodynamics**
Ad Agency: **Vicom/FCB**
Client: **Syntex**
Art Director: **Jeffrey Hicken**
Illustrator: **Thomas Slatkey (Paint Box Illustrator)**
Copywriter: **Janet Conley**
Model Maker: **Tony McVey**

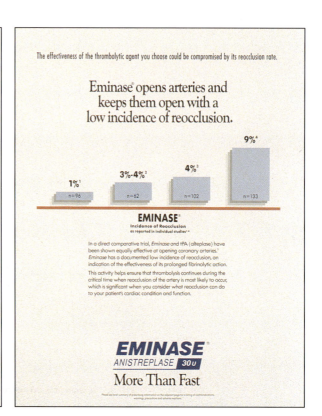

Product: **Eminase**
Title of Graphic: **Eminase Journal Ads**
Ad Agency: **Frank J. Corbett, Inc.**
Client: **SmithKline Beecham Pharmaceuticals/The Upjohn Company**
Art Director: **Linda Carpenter**
Photographer: **Don Levey**
Copywriter: **Joe Kuchta**

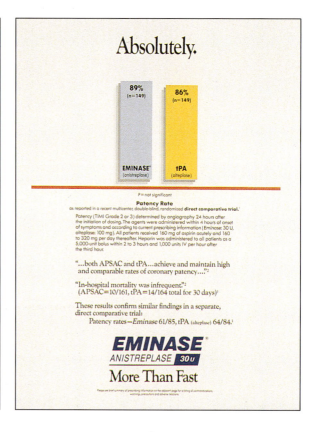

Space Advertising

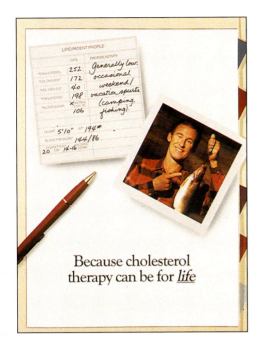

Product: **Questran**
Title of Graphic: **Questran Sales Aid**
Ad Agency: **Frank J. Corbett, Inc.**
Client: **Bristol-Myers Squibb U.S.P.D.**
Art Director: **Bill Reinwald**
Photographer: **Paul Elledge**
Copywriter: **Chris Weber**

Product: **The Meat Board**
Title of Graphic: **Breast of Chicken, Best of Pork**
Ad Agency: **Frank J. Corbett, Inc.**
Client: **National Live Stock and Meat Board**
Art Director: **Bill Reinwald**
Photographer: **Ken Ferguson**
Copywriter: **Karen Leavitt**

Space Advertising

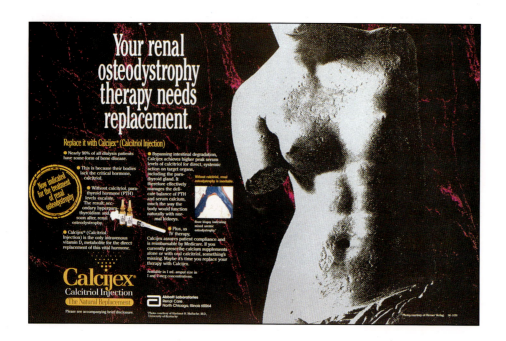

Product: **Calcijex**
Title of Graphic: **Calcijex Ad**
Ad Agency: **Gerbig Snell/Weisheimer & Associates**
Client: **Abbott Laboratories**
Art Director: **Jim Lutz**
Photographer: **Hirmer Verlag (Stock)**
Copywriter: **Elizabeth Ficocelli**

Product: **Blazing a Genetic Trail/A Report from the Howard Hughes Medical Institute**
Title of Graphic: **How To Conquer a Genetic Disease**
Design Firm: **RCW Communication Design Inc.**
Client: **Howard Hughes Medical Institute**
Art Director: **Rodney C. Williams**
Designer: **Leon Lawrence III**
Illustrator: **Stansbury Ronsaville Wood, Inc.**
Editor: **Maya Pines**
Editorial Director: **Robert A. Potter**

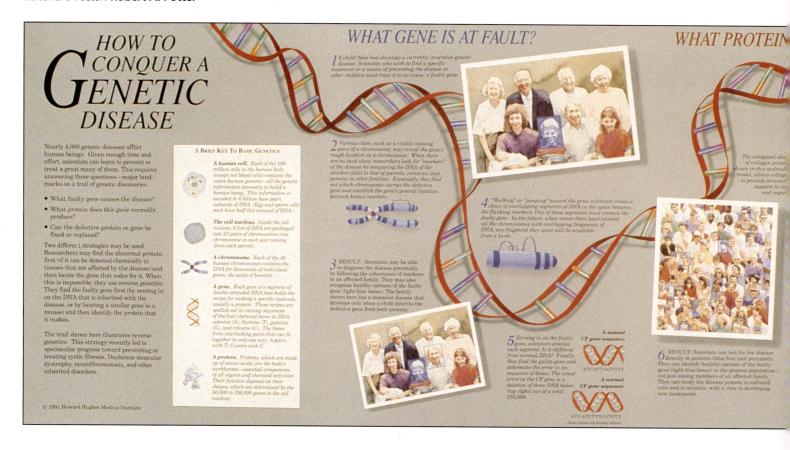

Space Advertising

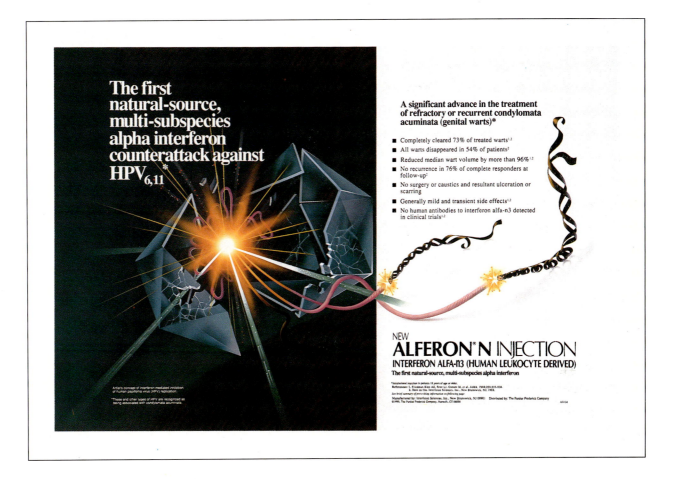

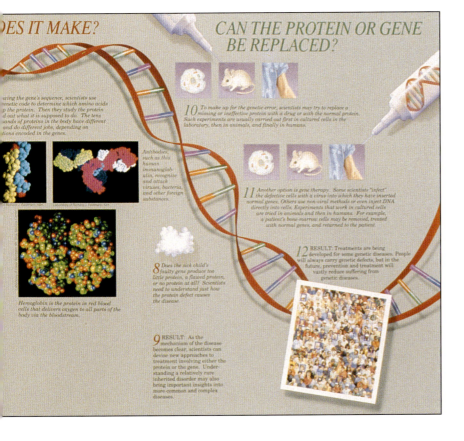

Product: **Alferon N Injection**
Title of Graphic: **Launch Ad**
Ad Agency: **Bryan, Brown & Malinsky**
Client: **The Purdue Frederick Company**
Art Director: **Richard Malinsky/Ralph Schwartz**
Illustrator: **Radu Vero**
Copywriter: **Donald Brown**

Space Advertising

 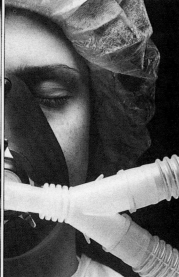 

Title of Graphic: **Are Patients' Drugs of Choice . . .**
Ad Agency: **J. Walter Thompson Healthcare Group**
Client: **Partnership for a Drug-Free America**
Art Director: **Steve Frederick**
Photographer: **Mike Raab**
Copywriter: **John Morris**

Title of Graphic: **How to Talk About Drug Abuse**
Ad Agency: **J. Walter Thompson Healthcare Group**
Client: **Partnership for a Drug-Free America**
Art Director: **Bob Levy**
Illustrator: **Bob Levy**
Copywriter: Jeff Mucciolo/Bob Levy

Space Advertising

Title of Graphic: **Helping John Unwind**
Ad Agency: **Kallir, Philips, Ross, Inc.**
Client: **Partnership for a Drug-Free America**
Art Director: **Bill Baffa**
Photographer: **Steve Spelman**
Copywriter: **Jack Henderson**J

Product: **Public Service Ad**
Title of Graphic: **Your Company may be Threatened by a Hostile Takeover Only You can Spot**
Ad Agency: **Sudler & Hennessey**
Client: **Partnership for a Drug-Free America**
Art Director: **Joe Chierchio**
Photographer: **Dennis Kitchen**
Copywriter: **John Chervokas**

Product: **Tribrissen**
Title of Graphic: **Veterinary Abscesses**
Ad Agency: **Howard Merrell & Partners**
Client: **Pitman-Moore, Inc.**
Art Director: **Susan Jones**
Illustrator: **Jane Hurd**
Copywriter: **Bob McQueen**

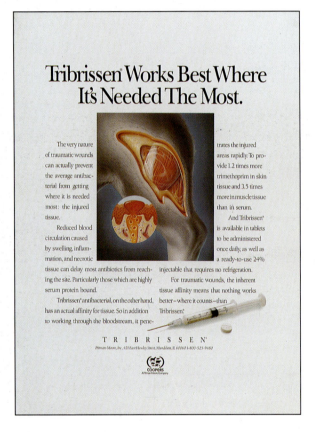

Product: **Tribrissen**
Title of Graphic: **Veterinary Traumatic Wounds**
Ad Agency: **Howard Merrell & Partners**
Client: **Pitman-Moore, Inc.**
Art Director: **Susan Jones**
Illustrator: **Jane Hurd**
Copywriter: **Bob McQueen**

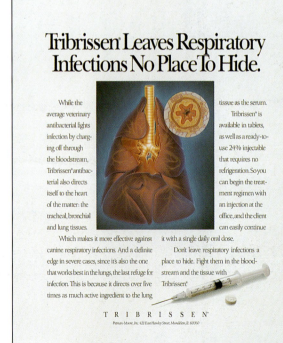

Product: **Tribrissen**
Title of Graphic: **Veterinary Respiratory Infections**
Ad Agency: **Howard Merrell & Partners**
Client: **Pitman-Moore, Inc.**
Art Director: **Susan Jones**
Illustrator: **Jane Hurd**
Copywriter: **Bob McQueen**

DIRECT MAIL

Direct mail affords distinct advantages over traditional "nonpersonal" ads. Mail can target a specific audience and deliver a personalized message. The first objective for any mail piece is to get delivered. The next greatest achievement is to get opened, especially in the crowded and competitive environment that exists. The greatest success of any mail piece is to get read. The triumph of any mail piece is to either have quantifiable results from readership (via a response mechanism) or establish a dialogue between the company and the customer. This section demonstrates some highly effective mail pieces that got delivered, got read, and got results.

Direct Mail

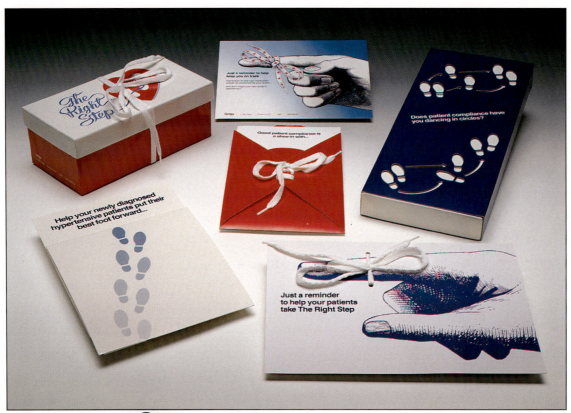

Product: **Lopresser**
Title of Graphic: **The Right Step**
Ad Agency: **C & G Advertising Agency, Inc.**
Client: **Ciba-Geigy Pharmaceuticals**
Art Director: **Loren Mork**
Illustrator: **Tom Carnase**
Copywriter: **Kevin Purcell**
Structural Designer: **Trimensions, Inc.**

Product: **Cyclocort**
Title of Graphic: **Response Ability Fax Mailer**
Ad Agency: **Dugan/Farley Communications**
Client: **Lederle Laboratories**
Art Director: **Daniel W. Smith**
Illustrator: **Tony Randazzo**
Copywriter: **Marcia Blaustein/Dave Schroeder**
Structural Designer: **Structural Graphics**

Direct Mail

Product: **Lupron Depot**
Title of Graphic: **Escape from Endo**
Ad Agency: **Botto, Roessner, Horne & Messinger**
Client: **Tap Pharmaceuticals**
Art Director: **Hector Padron**
Illustrator: **William T. Major**
Copywriter: **Cathy Popescu**

Direct Mail

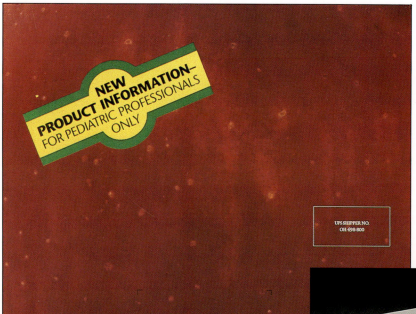

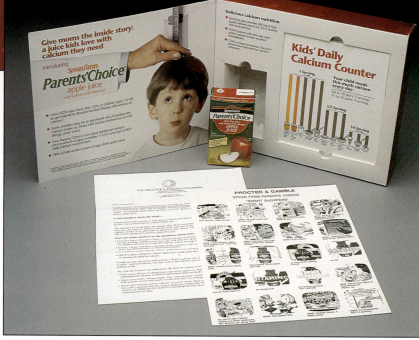

Product: **Speas Farm Parent Choice Apple Juice**
Title of Graphic: **Direct Mail #10**
Ad Agency: **Gross Townsend Frank Hoffman**
Client: **Proctor & Gamble**
Art Director: **Dave Frank/Caroline Waloski**
Photographer: **Jeff Morgan**
Copywriter: **Ronnie Hoffman**

Product: **Nasalcrom**
Title of Graphic: **Allergy Season is Here**
Ad Agency: **Sandler Communications**
Client: **Fisons Pharmaceuticals**
Art Director: **Lori Mulhern**
Illustrator: **Jack Davis**
Copywriter: **Lisa Stec**

Direct Mail

Product: **Anaprox DS**
Title of Graphic: **Anaprox DS Dental Mailers**
Ad Agency: **Baxter, Gurian and Mazzei, Inc.**
Client: **Syntex**
Art Director: **Don Kapp**
Photographer: **Tom Keller**
Copywriter: **Bill Melhourn**

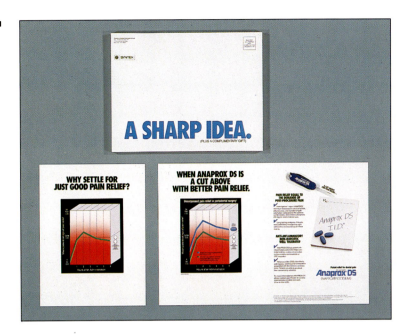

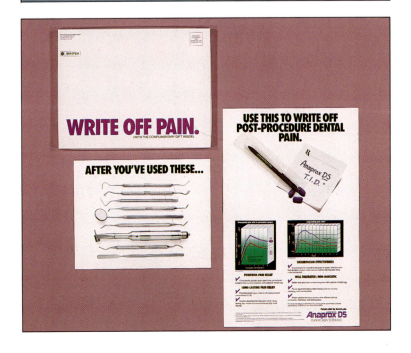

Direct Mail

Product: **Maxzide**
Title of Graphic: **Senior Challenge**
Ad Agency: **The LeDA Agency**
Client: **Lederle Laboratories**
Art Director: **Bruce Walk**
Illustrator: **Dee Dee Burnside**
Copywriter: **Jean Allan**
Structural Designer: **TriAd**

Direct Mail

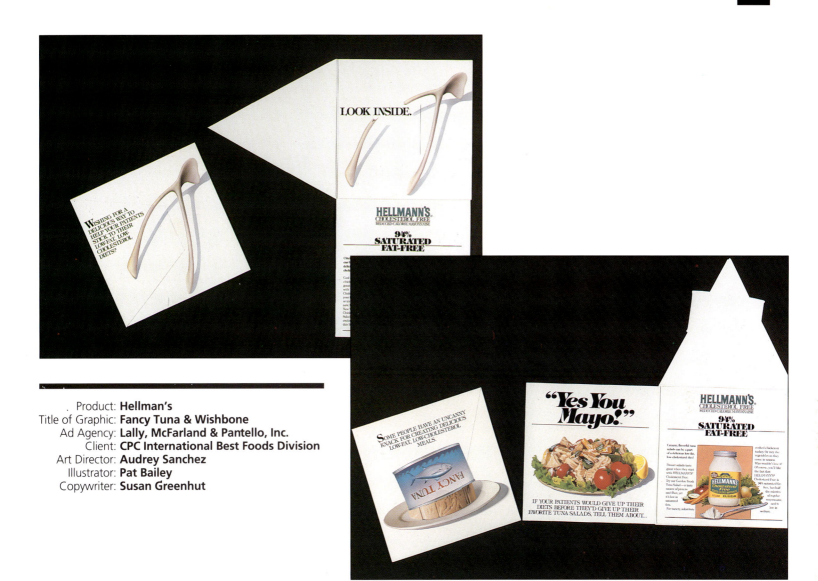

Product: **Hellman's**
Title of Graphic: **Fancy Tuna & Wishbone**
Ad Agency: **Lally, McFarland & Pantello, Inc.**
Client: **CPC International Best Foods Division**
Art Director: **Audrey Sanchez**
Illustrator: **Pat Bailey**
Copywriter: **Susan Greenhut**

Product: **Algitec**
Title of Graphic: **Campaign**
Ad Agency: **McCann-Erickson Manchester**
Client: **SmithKline Beecham Pharmaceuticals**
Art Director: **Paul Pomfret**
Photographer: **Tyger Tyger Photography**
Copywriter: **Lisa Middlehurst**

Direct Mail

Product: **Benadryl Elixir**
Title of Graphic: **Inside: The Allergy Expert Comes to Your Waiting Room!**
Ad Agency: **Sudler & Hennessey**
Client: **Parke-Davis Consumer Health Products Group**
Art Director: **Siu Yuen Chan**
Illustrator: **Tom Huffman**
Copywriter: **Sandra Holtzman**

Product: **Benadryl Decongestant Elixir**
Title of Graphic: **A Gift for You from the Allergy Expert — Inside!**
Ad Agency: **Sudler & Hennessey**
Client: **Parke-Davis Consumer Health Products Group**
Art Director: **Siu Yuen Chan**
Illustrator: **Tom Huffman/Sabrina Chin**
Copywriter: **Sandra Holtzman**

Direct Mail

Product: **Voltaren**
Title of Graphic: **3-D Mailing Box**
Ad Agency: **Salthouse, Torre, Norton**
Client: **Ciba-Geigy**
Art Director: **Mike Lazur, Juan Ramos**
Illustrator: **Clockwork Apple**
Photographer: **Carmine Macedonia**
Copywriter: **Peter Chamedes**
Structural Designer: **Trimensions, Inc.**

Product: **Ciba-Geigy Managed Healthcare Services**
Title of Graphic: **Put Your Best Foot Forward . . .**
Ad Agency: **C & G Advertising Agency, Inc.**
Client: **Ciba-Geigy Managed Healthcare Services**
Art Director: **Varsha Mehta**
Photographer: **George Diebold**
Copywriter: **John Lewis**

Product: **Ciba-Geigy Managed Healthcare Services**
Title of Graphic: **You Are Invited . . .**
Ad Agency: **C & G Advertising Agency, Inc.**
Client: **Ciba-Geigy Managed Healthcare Services**
Art Director: **Varsha Mehta**
Copywriter: **John Lewis**
Illustrator: **Steve Martin**

Direct Mail

Product: **Datascope Monitors**
Title of Graphic: **SaO2 Monitor-Line Mailer**
Ad Agency: **Dick Jackson, Inc.**
Client: **Datascope Corp.**
Art Director: **David Lukshus**
Photographer: **Ralph Massullo**
Copywriter: **Richard Jackson**

Product: **Laser Plume Face Mask**
Title of Graphic: **We've Changed our Color**
Ad Agency: **Pierce-Davis & Associates**
Client: **Johnson & Johnson Medical, Inc.**
Art Director: **Pam Gampper, Bill Galyean**
Illustrator: **Don Punchatz**
Copywriter: **Margie Bowles**

Direct Mail

Product: **Floxin**
Title of Graphic: **Nostalgia Along the Nile**
Ad Agency: **Botto, Roessner, Horne & Messinger**
Client: **Ortho Pharmaceutical Corp.**
Art Director: **Hector Padron**
Illustrator: **Joel A. Leuine**
Copywriter: **Susan Roessner/Cathy Popescu**

Direct Mail

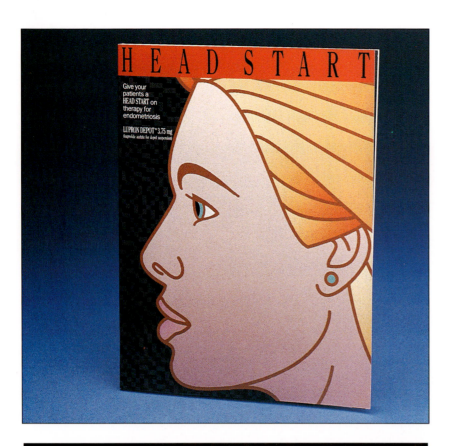

Product: **Lupron 3.75**
Title of Graphic: **Headstart: Where the Management of Endometriosis Begins**
Ad Agency: **Abelson-Taylor, Inc.**
Client: **TAP Pharmaceuticals, Inc.**
Art Director: **Jay Doniger/Stephen Neale**
Illustrator: **Mark Jasin/Bill Graham Studio**
Copywriter: **Jeff Chouinard**

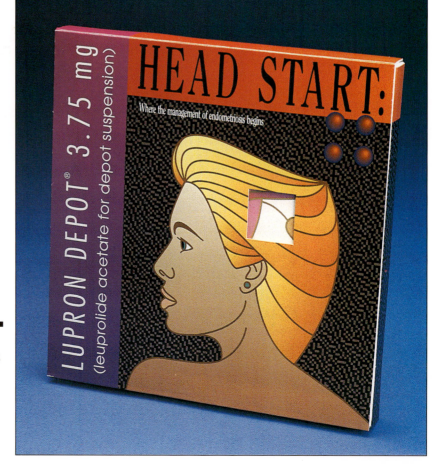

Product: **Lupron 3.75**
Title of Graphic: **Headstart on Therapy for Endometriosis**
Ad Agency: **Abelson-Taylor, Inc.**
Client: **TAP Pharmaceuticals, Inc.**
Art Director: **Jay Doniger/Stephen Neale**
Illustrator: **Mark Jasin/Bill Graham Studio**
Copywriter: **Jeff Chouinard**

Direct Mail

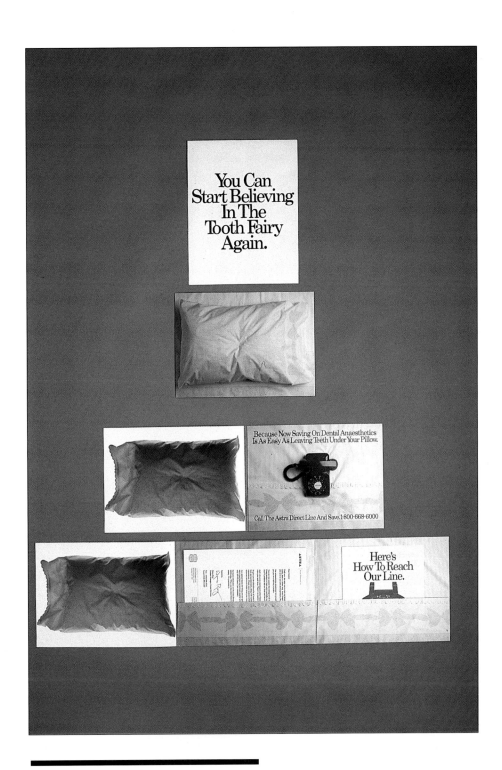

Product: **Astra Dental Products**
Title of Graphic: **You can Start Believing . . .**
Ad Agency: **SMW Advertising**
Client: **Astra Pharm., Inc.**
Art Director: **Scott Dube**
Photographer: **Dave Sloan**
Copywriter: **Karen Levenson**

Direct Mail

Product: **PAC Christmas Card**
Title of Graphic: **PAC Christmas**
Ad Agency: **Lavey/Wolff/Swift**
Art Director: **Ken Lavey**
Illustrator: **Peter Taylor**
Copywriter: **Michael Metelenis**
Structural Designer: **PAC**

Product: **Calcimar (calcitonin-salmon)**
Title of Graphic: **Salmon Series**
Ad Agency: **Thomas G. Ferguson Associates, Inc.**
Client: **Rhone-Poulenc Rorer**
Art Director: **Nancy Schroeter**
Photographer: **Linda Bohm**
Illustrator: **Terry Palmer**
Structural Designer: **Structural Graphics**

Direct Mail

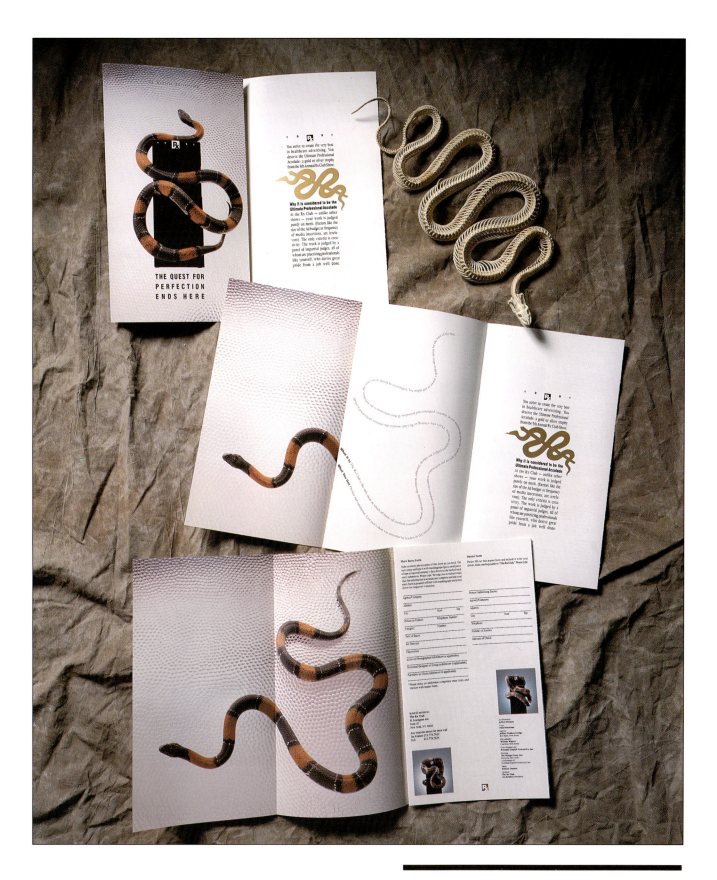

Product: **The Rx Club Call for Entries**
Title of Graphic: **The Rx Club Call for Entries Mailer**
Design Firm: **Jeffrey Pienkos Design**
Client: **The Rx Club**
Art Director: **Jeffrey Pienkos**
Photographer: **William Wagner Photography**
Copywriter: **Nina Padukone**
Structural Designer: **Ave M. Lindon**

Direct Mail

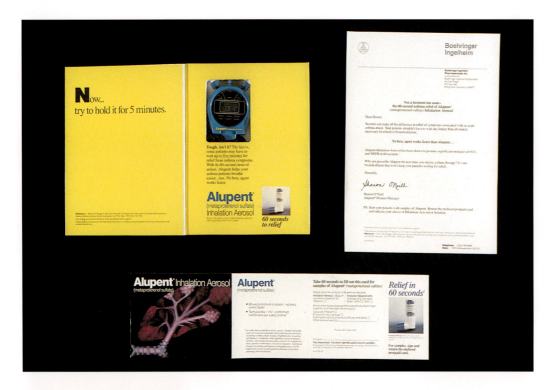

Product: **Alupent**
Title of Graphic: **Alupent Mail Campaign**
Ad Agency: **Gross Townsend Frank Hoffman**
Client: **Boeringer Inglehiem**
Art Director: **Orin Kimball**
Copywriter: **Dana Delibovi**
Structural Designer: **Lee Klein Associates**

Direct Mail

95

Product: **Loxitane loxapine succinate**
Title of Graphic: **Loxitane Ship Series**
Ad Agency: **LeDA Agency**
Client: **Lederle Laboratories**
Art Director: **Scott Tanelli**
Illustrator: **Dennis Recchia**
Copywriter: **Jean Allan**
Structural Designer: **Intervisual Communications**

Product: **Asendin (amoxapine)**
Title of Graphic: **Asendin Critical Cases**
Ad Agency: **LeDA Agency**
Client: **Lederle Laboratories**
Art Director: **Scott Tanelli**
Photographer: **Bill Wagner**
Copywriter: **Jean Allan**

Direct Mail

Product: **Clozaril (clozapine)**
Title of Graphic: **Portrait of Success**
Ad Agency: **M.E.D. Communications**
Client: **Sandoz Pharmaceuticals**
Art Director: **Jim Crispo**
Photographer: **Rich Russo/Dennis Kitchen**
Copywriter: **Jack Speiller/Mike Brune**
Structural Designer: **Innotech/Structural Graphics/Thebault**

Product: **Clozaril (clozapine)**
Title of Graphic: **Portrait of Success**
Ad Agency: **M.E.D. Communications**
Client: **Sandoz Pharmaceuticals**
Art Director: **Jim Crispo**
Photographer: **Rich Russo/Dennis Kitchen**
Copywriter: **Jack Speiller/Mike Brune**
Structural Designer: **Innotech/Structural Graphics/Thebault**

Product: **Clozaril (clozapine)**
Title of Graphic: **Portrait of Success**
Ad Agency: **M.E.D. Communications**
Client: **Sandoz Pharmaceuticals**
Art Director: **Jim Crispo**
Photographer: **Rich Russo/Dennis Kitchen**
Copywriter: **Jack Speiller/Mike Brune**
Structural Designer: **Innotech/Structural Graphics/Thebault**

Direct Mail

97

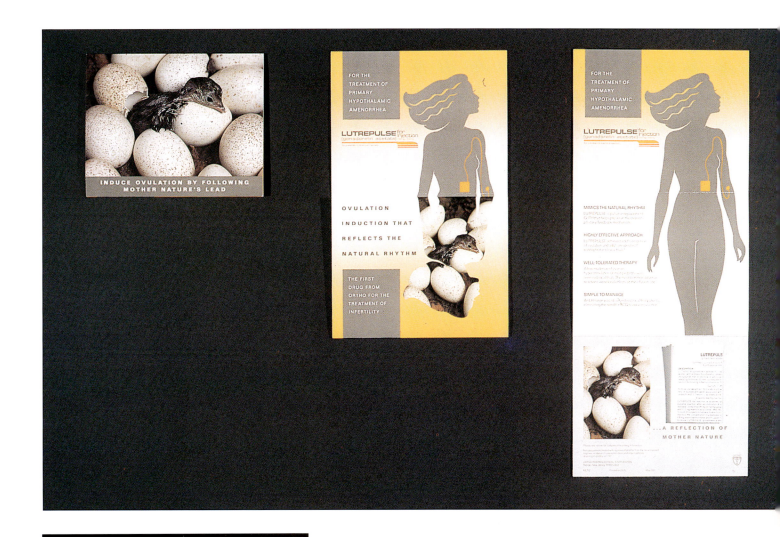

Product: **Estraderm**
Title of Graphic: **Estraderm Information Unit**
Ad Agency: **Dugan/Farley Communications**
Client: **Ciba-Geigy**
Art Director: **Suzanne Elward**
Copywriter: **Martin Ross**
Structural Designer: **Trimensions, Inc.**

Product: **Lutrepulse**
Title of Graphic: **Natural Rhythm — Mother Nature's Lead**
Ad Agency: **Kallir, Philips, Ross, Inc.**
Client: **Ortho Pharmaceuticals**
Art Director: **Miriam Freedman/Jeff Lubalin**
Photographer: **Marcia Griffen/Animals Animals**
Copywriter: **Carol Gorman**

Direct Mail

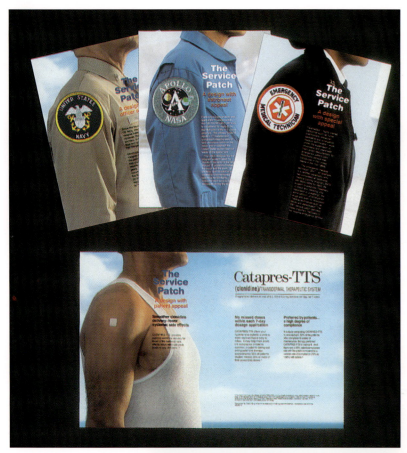

Product: **Catapress-TTS**
Title of Graphic: **Service Patch Mail Series**
Ad Agency: **Barnum & Souza, Inc.**
Client: **Boehringer Ingelheim Pharmaceuticals, Inc.**
Art Director: **David Barnum**
Photographer: **Skip Hine**
Copywriter: **Carla Olinger**

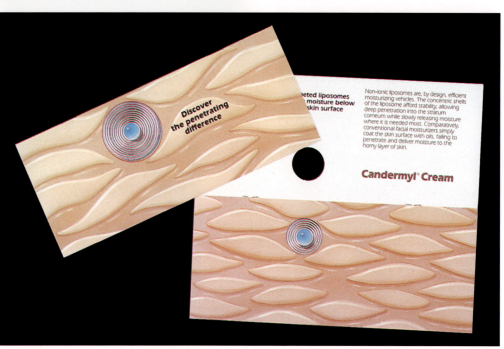

Product: **Norgesic Forte**
Title of Graphic: **It Can't be Done Alone**
Ad Agency: **Girgenti, Hughes, Butler & McDowell**
Client: **3M Pharmaceuticals**
Art Director: **Mark McDowell**
Photographer: **Marc David Cohen**
Copywriter: **Bob Ranieri**

Direct Mail

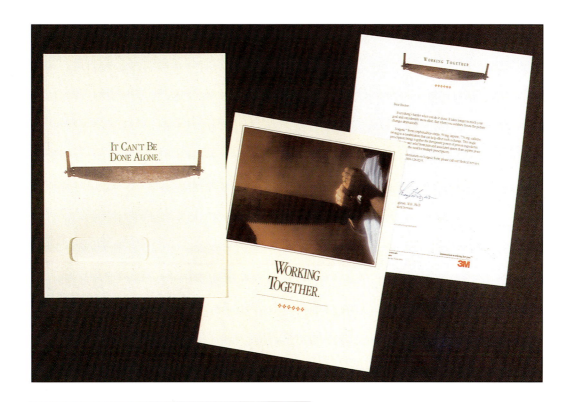

Product: **Norgesic Forte**
Title of Graphic: **It Can't be Done Alone**
Ad Agency: **Girgenti, Hughes, Butler & McDowell**
Client: **3M Pharmaceuticals**
Art Director: **Mark McDowell**
Photographer: **Marc David Cohen**
Copywriter: **Bob Ranieri**

Product: **Micronase (Glyburide)**
Title of Graphic: **The Sugar-Free Free Offer**
Ad Agency: **Kallir, Philips, Ross, Inc.**
Client: **The Upjohn Company**
Art Director: **James Burton**
Illustrator: **Seymour Chwast**
Copywriter: **Joanne H. Dalton**

Direct Mail

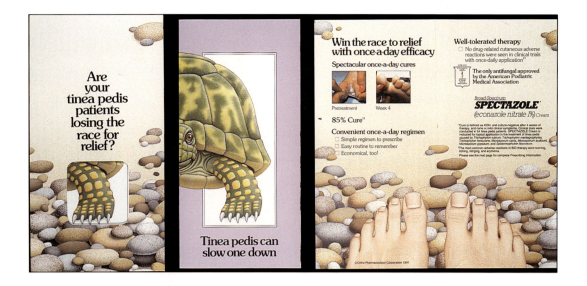

Product: **Spectazole**
Title of Graphic: **Fungal Jungle**
Ad Agency: **Kallir, Philips, Ross, Inc.**
Client: **Ortho Dermatological Division**
Art Director: **Maureen Hutchinson**
Illustrator: **Ben Luce**
Copywriter: **Carol Gorman**

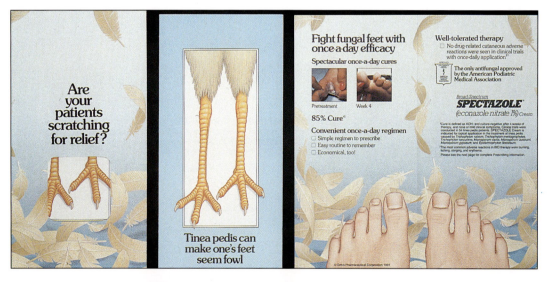

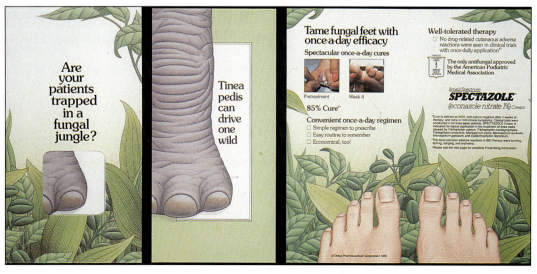

Direct Mail

Product: **Vaseline Intensive Care Sun Screen**
Title of Graphic: **Spring is Stronger than You Think**
Ad Agency: **Sudler & Hennessey**
Client: **Chesebrough-Ponds, Inc.**
Art Director: **Marie Krajan**
Illustrator: **Air Studio**
Copywriter: **Tim Millas**
Structural Designer: **Packaging Trends**

Product: **Trilisate (choline magnesium trilisate) and Betadine First Aid Cream**
Title of Graphic: **Send Patients Home on a Faster Track**
Ad Agency: **William Douglas McAdams, Inc.**
Client: **Purdue Fredericks Company**
Art Director: **Patrick Creaven/Diane Lynch**
Photographer: **Shig Ikeda**
Copywriter: **Gwenne Frieman**

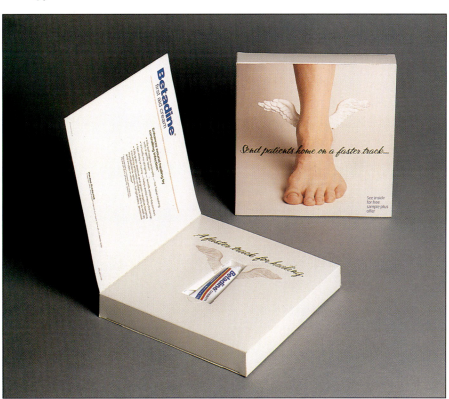

Direct Mail

Product: **Anaprox DS**
Title of Graphic: **When You Hear Voice Chip Mailer**
Ad Agency: **Baxter, Gurian and Mazzei, Inc.**
Client: **Syntex Laboratories**
Art Director: **Alan Ichiriu**
Photographer: **Glen Wexler**
Copywriter: **Bill Melhourn**
Structural Designer: **Structural Graphics**

Product: **Loprox**
Title of Graphic: **Loprox Foot Soldiers**
Ad Agency: **Gerbig Snell/Weisheimer & Associates**
Client: **Hoechst-Roussel Pharmaceuticals**
Art Director: **Diane Hay**
Photographer: **Morton & White**
Copywriter: **Amy Dimon**

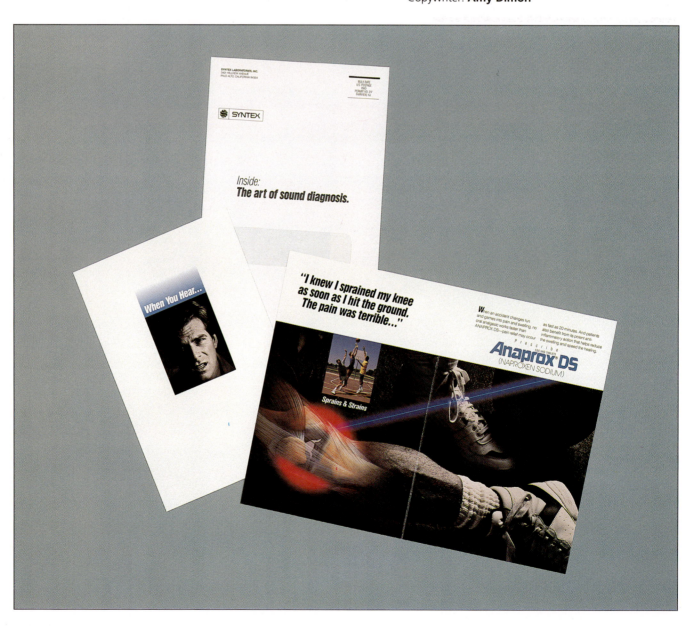

Direct Mail

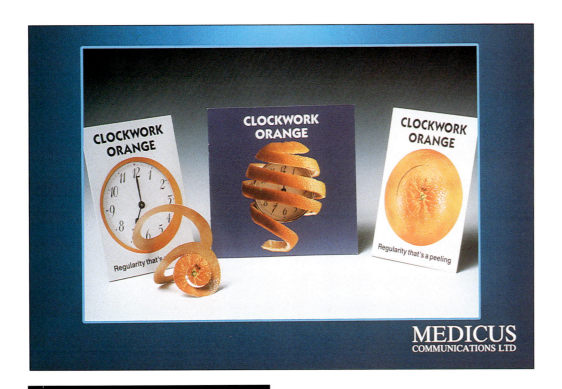

Product: **Fybogel Orange**
Title of Graphic: **Clockwork Orange Mailing**
Ad Agency: **Medicus Communications Ltd.**
Client: **Reckitt & Colman**
Art Director: **Shirley Hart/Shelanne Dickie**
Illustrator: **Geoff Pike**
Photographer: **Jay Myrdal**
Copywriter: **Jacqui Hogan**

Product: **Voltaren**
Title of Graphic: **Anatomical Models**
Design Firm: **Trimensions, Inc.**
Client: **Ciba-Geigy**
Art Director: **Cliff Wood**
Structural Designer: **Trimensions, Inc.**

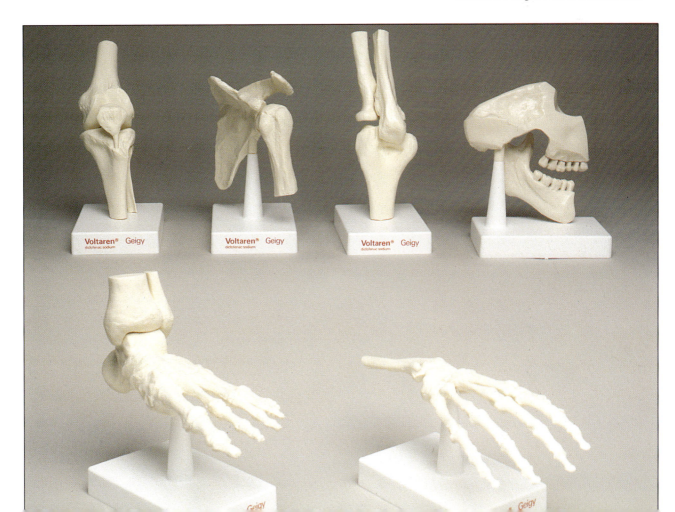

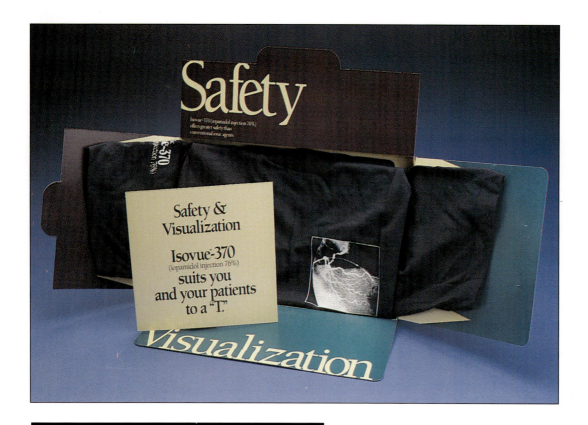

Product: **Isovue**
Title of Graphic: **Safety and Visualization Phase 2**
Ad Agency: **Abelson-Taylor, Inc.**
Client: **Squibb Diagnostics**
Art Director: **Jay Doniger/Stephen Neale**
Copywriter: **Rich Kellner**
Structural Designer: **Chapco**

Product: **Aoesept Disinfection/Neutralization Solution**
Ad Agency: **Dorland Sweeney Jones**
Client: **Ciba Vision Corp.**
Art Director: **Ron Lewis**
Photographer: **Kevin Black, Randy Duchaine, Walter Hodges**
Copywriter: **Reid Goldsborough**
Structural Designer: **Packaging Network**

Direct Mail

Product: **Mexitil (Mexiletine HCl)**
Title of Graphic: **Consider The Risks in a Hazardous Environment**
Ad Agency: **Dugan/Farley Communications**
Client: **Boehringer Ingelheim Pharmaceuticals, Inc.**
Art Director: **Suzanne Elward**
Illustrator: **Rich Grote**
Photographer: **Vince Marchese**
Copywriter: **Frank Cordasco**
Structural Designer: **Printcom**

Direct Mail

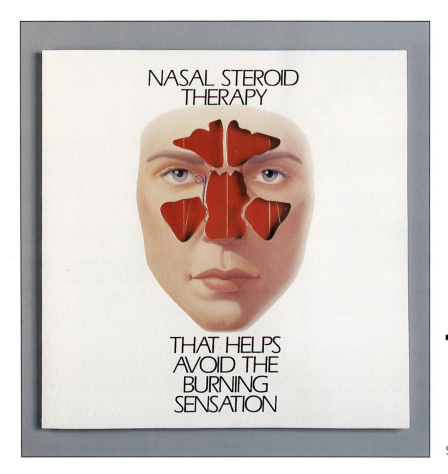

Product: **Vancenase AQ**
Title of Graphic: **Nasal Steroid Therapy**
Ad Agency: **William Douglas McAdams, Inc.**
Client: **Schering**
Art Director: **Haig Adishian**
Illustrator: **Jane Hurd**
Copywriter: **Claire Hakun/James Vespe**
Structural Designer: **Structural Graphics**

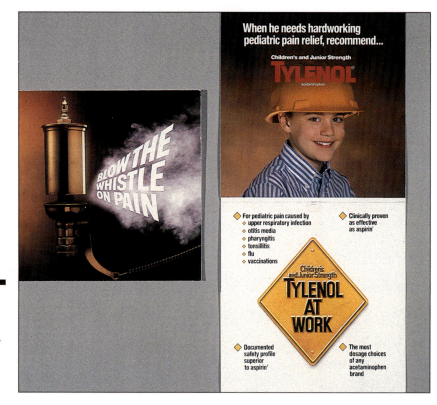

Product: **Children's Tylenol**
Title of Graphic: **Blow the Whistle on Pain**
Ad Agency: **Kallir, Philips, Ross, Inc.**
Client: **McNeil Consumer Products Company**
Art Director: **Annette Ricciardi/Nina Wachsman**
Photographer: **John Manno/Susan Richman**
Copywriter: **Lorraine McNeill-Popper**

Direct Mail

Product: **Slo-Bid**
Title of Graphic: **Think Big**
Ad Agency: **Thomas G. Ferguson Associates**
Client: **Rhone-Doulenc Rorer Pharmaceuticals, Inc.**
Art Director: **Jeff Lipman/John Quinn**
Photographer: **John Emerson**
Copywriter: **Joe Gattuso**
Structural Designer: **Trimensions, Inc.**

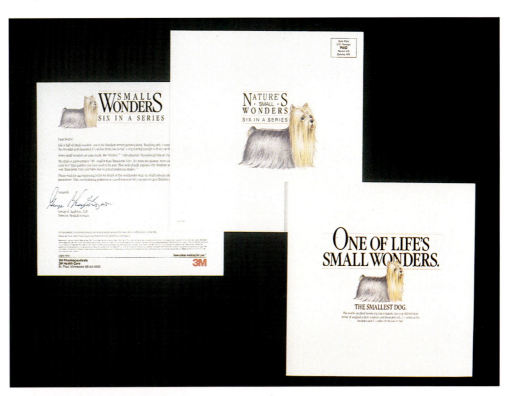

Product: **Minitran**
Title of Graphic: **Small Wonders**
Ad Agency: **Girgenti, Hughes, Butler & McDowell**
Client: **3M Pharmaceuticals**
Art Director: **Mark McDowell**
Illustrator: **Sharon Ellis**
Copywriter: **Frank Hughes**

Direct Mail

Product: **ConvaTec, Closed End Ostomy Pouches**
Title of Graphic: **Closed End Case History**
Ad Agency: **Gross Townsend Frank Hoffman**
Client: **Bristol-Meyers/Squibb**
Art Director: **Jeff Turner**
Photographer: **Katrina Filary**
Copywriter: **Alan Rothenberg**

Product: **Isoptin SR**
Title of Graphic: **Less of a Good Thing**
Ad Agency: **Blunt Hann Sersen, Inc.**
Client: **Knoll Pharmaceuticals**
Art Director: **Jeff Lipman**
Copywriter: **Karen Blunt/Dave Biro**

SALES PROMOTION

For simplicity's sake it may be said that the goal of an ad is to sell, and that the goal of a direct mail piece is to deliver a specific message to a targeted population and generate a response. In similarly simple terms, the goal of sales promotion is to attract attention and jog memory. Promotional items can run the gamut from educational or clinical items to corporate or product brochures. Once limited only by budget and imagination, a new regulatory sensitivity has begun to color much of this type of promotion. This section includes diverse examples — from logo design to selling aids — that share the greatest common denominator: creativity that transcends constraint.

Sales Promotion

Help your patients button up without morning stiffness.

Pick up
this button
for help.

Feldene® (piroxicam) relieves the morning stiffness of arthritis.

Buttoning a shirt, sweater or dress are just some of the obstacles facing the arthritis patient with morning stiffness. Once-daily FELDENE relieves arthritis symptoms around the clock,[1] allowing patients to sleep better,[1] awaken with less morning stiffness[2] and perform daily activities better.[3]

Helps Your Arthritis Patients Wake Up to Good Mornings

Please see next page for brief summary of FELDENE® (piroxicam) prescribing information.
© 1989, Pfizer Inc. 1989 Turner Entertainment Co. All Rights Reserved 1938 Loews Inc. Ren. 1966 MGM

Product: **Feldene**
Title of Graphic: **Pick it Up Ads — Key, Button, Coin**
Ad Agency: **Dorritie Lyons & Nickel**
Client: **Pfizer Pharmaceuticals**
Art Director: **Mike Lyons**
Photographer: **Carl Flatow**
Copywriter: **Bill Brown**

Product: **Procardia**
Ad Agency: **Dorritie Lyons & Nickel**
Client: **Pfizer Pharmaceuticals**
Art Director: **Tom Velardi**
Photographer: **Bob Walsh**
Copywriter: **Carol Shepko**

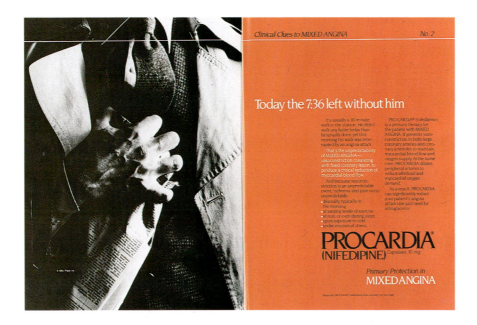

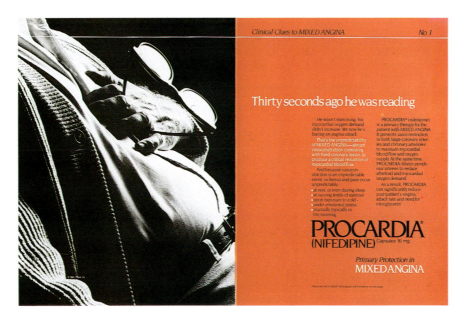

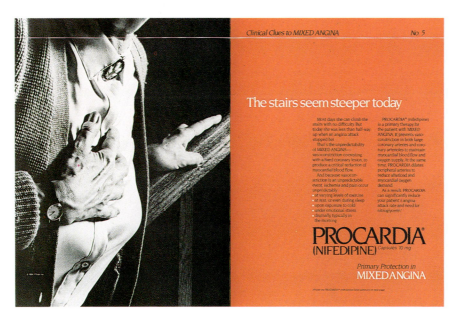

Sales Promotion

S SILVER

Product: **Tagamet**
Title of Graphic: **IRS Audit**
Ad Agency: **Salthouse Torre Norton, Inc.**
Client: **SmithKline Beecham Pharmaceutical**
Art Director: **William C. Beauchamp**
Photographer: **William Wagner**
Copywriter: **Chuck Dexter**

Product: **Tagamet**
Title of Graphic: **3:15 a.m.**
Ad Agency: **Salthouse Torre Norton, Inc.**
Client: **SmithKline Beecham Pharmaceutical**
Art Director: **Jeffrey Pienkos**
Illustrator: **Steve Heimann**
Copywriter: **Mike Norton/Doug Baron**

S SILVER

Product: **Carafate**
Title of Graphic: **Carafate Protective Maintenance Tool Box**
Ad Agency: **Abelson-Taylor Inc.**
Client: **Marion Merrell Dow**
Art Director: **Stephen Neale**
Illustrator: **Bill Graham Studios**
Copywriter: **Jeff Chouinard**

Sales Promotion

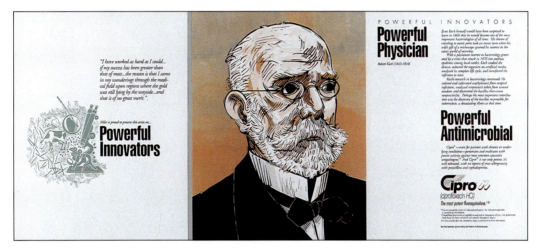

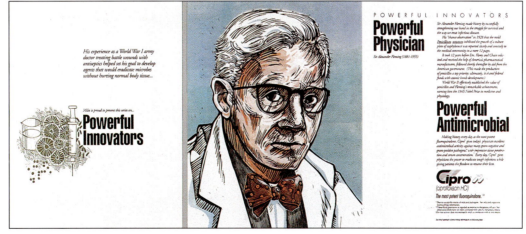

Product: **Cipro**
Title of Graphic: **Cipro Powerful Innovators**
Design Firm: **Lavey/Wolff/Swift**
Client: **Miles Inc.**
Art Director: **Ken Lavey**
Illustrator: **Norman Gorbaty**
Copywriter: **Michael Metelenis**

Sales Promotion

Product: **Cherry Creme Extra Strength Maalox Plus**
Title of Graphic: **Cherry Crate**
Ad Agency: **Kallir, Philips, Ross, Inc.**
Client: **Rorer Pharmaceutical Corp.**
Art Director: **Deborah Maguire**
Illustrator: **Jim Meehan**
Photographer: **John Manno**
Copywriter: **Lorraine McNeill-Popper**

Product: **KPR Self-Promo**
Title of Graphic: **We're Opening New Windows**
Ad Agency: **Kallir, Philips, Ross, Inc.**
Art Director: **Al Zalon, Fran Elfenbein**
Photographer: **Bernard Lawrence**
Copywriter: **John Kallir, Phyllis Wachsman**

Sales Promotion

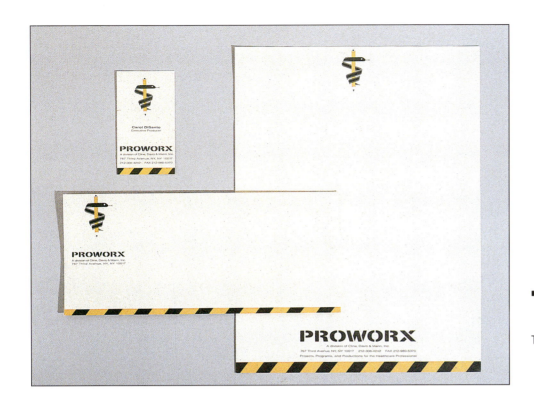

Product: **Proworx, a division of Cline, Davis & Mann, Inc.**
Title of Graphic: **Letterhead & Business Card**
Ad Agency: **Cline, Davis & Mann, Inc.**
Client: **Proworx**
Art Director: **Andy Moore**

Product: **Ansaid**
Title of Graphic: **Joint Communique Views**
Ad Agency: **Pracon**
Client: **The Upjohn Company**
Art Director: **Al Halac**
Illustrator: **Tim Buffaloe**
Copywriter: **Mara Adams**
Structural Designer: **Carol I. Iglesias**

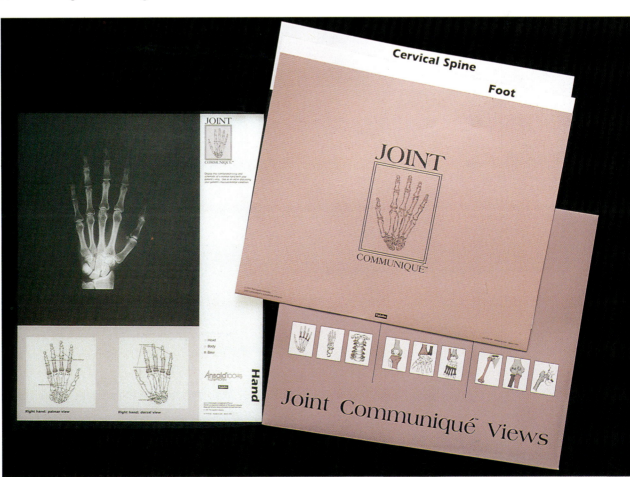

Sales Promotion

Title of Graphic: **Viral Hepatitis Educators Conference**
Ad Agency: **Pracon**
Client: **Schering-Plough Pharmaceuticals**
Art Director: **Al Halac**
Illustrator: **Tomo Narashima**
Copywriter: **Terry Gruber-Tapsoba**
Structural Designer: **Carol I. Iglesias**

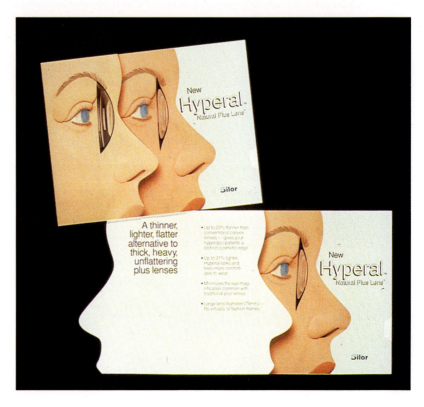

Product: **Hyperal Natural Plus Lens**
Title of Graphic: **Hyperal Natural Plus Lens**
Ad Agency: **Dugan/Farley Communications**
Client: **Silor, Division of Essilor of America**
Art Director: **Eric Rathje**
Illustrator: **Jonathon Milne**
Photographer: **Bernie Gold**
Copywriter: **Maureen Card**
Structural Designer: **Eric Rathje**

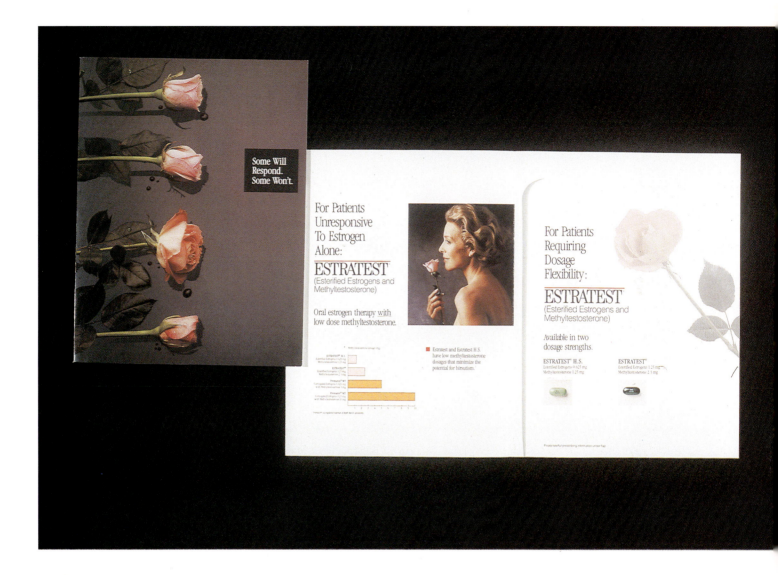

Product: **Estrotest**
Title of Graphic: **Some will Respond**
Ad Agency: **Girgenti, Hughes, Butler & McDowell**
Client: **Solvay**
Art Director: **Mark McDowell**
Photographer: **Marc Cohen**
Copywriter: **Frank Hughes**

Sales Promotion

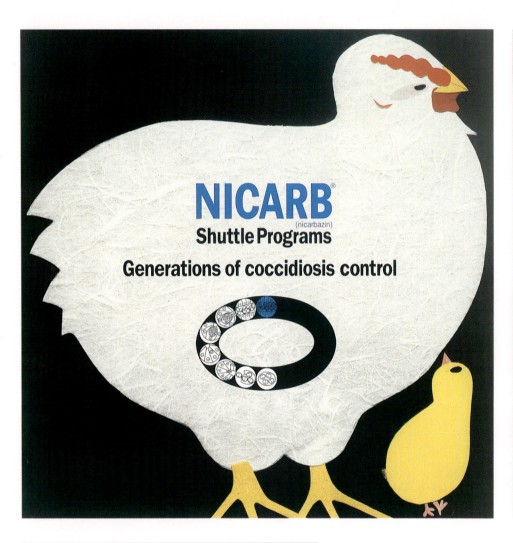

Product: **Nicarb**
Title of Graphic: **Nicarb Shuttle Programs**
Ad Agency: **Warhaftig Associates, Inc.**
Client: **MSD Agvet Division of Merck & Co., Inc.**
Art Director: **Reiner Lubge**
Illustrator: **Reiner Lubge**
Photographer: **Larry Lefever**
Copywriter: **Jonathan Hughes**

Product: **Uniphyl (theophylline, anhydrous)**
Title of Graphic: **Tame the Predator**
Ad Agency: **William Douglas McAdams, Inc.**
Client: **Purdue Fredericks Company**
Art Director: **Diane Lynch/Patrick Creaven**
Illustrator: **Ed Acuna**
Copywriter: **Gwenne Frieman**

Sales Promotion

Product: **Zestoretic**
Title of Graphic: **Mailing**
Ad Agency: **McCann-Erickson Manchester**
Client: **ICI Pharmaceuticals**
Art Director: **Steve Jones**
Illustrator: **Bill Worthington**
Copywriter: **Steve Mees**

Product: **Zoladex**
Title of Graphic: **Detail Aid**
Ad Agency: **McCann-Erickson Manchester**
Client: **ICI Pharmaceuticals**
Art Director: **Carole Davids**
Illustrator: **Carole Davids**
Photographer: **The Image Bank**
Copywriter: **Carol Thompson**

Sales Promotion

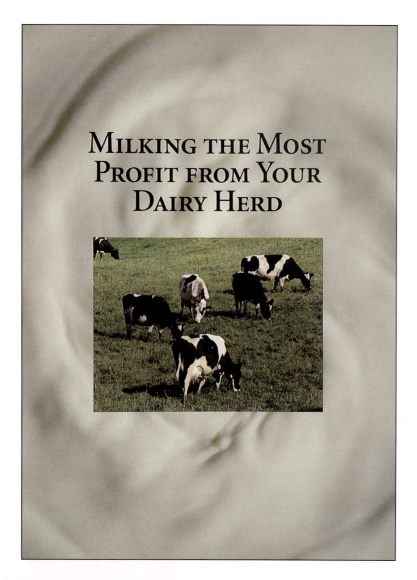

Product: **Ivomec, Corid, and TBZ**
Title of Graphic: **Milking the Most Profit from Your Dairy Herd**
Ad Agency: **Warhaftig Associates, Inc.**
Client: **MSD Agvet Division of Merck & Co., Inc.**
Art Director: **Matt Warhaftig**
Illustrator: **Michael Reingold**
Photographer: **Grant Heilman Photography, Inc.**
Copywriter: **Jonathan Hughes**

Product: **Zantac**
Title of Graphic: **Silent Partners in Many Patients**
Ad Agency: **Williams Douglas McAdams, Inc.**
Client: **Glaxo Pharmaceuticals**
Art Director: **Susan Fender**
Illustrator: **Lenny Anselmo/Jeff Holewski**
Copywriter: **Gwenne Frieman**

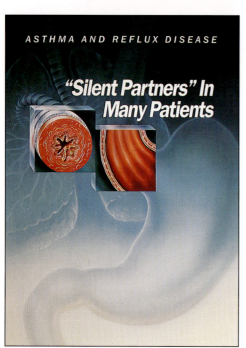

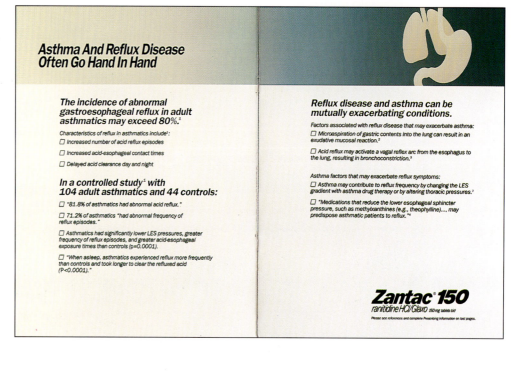

Sales Promotion

Product: **Gastrocrom**
Title of Graphic: **Medical Mystery Series**
Design Firm: **Sandler Communications**
Client: **Fisons Pharmaceuticals**
Art Director: **Adam Cohen**
Photographer: **Steve Lesnick**
Copywriter: **Tomo Asanovic**

Product: **Oncology**
Title of Graphic: **Hope Through Research**
Ad Agency: **LeDA Agency**
Client: **Lederle Laboratories**
Art Director: **Bruce Walk**
Illustrator: **Evin Del Moro**

Sales Promotion

Product: **Uresil**
Title of Graphic: **Joining Technology and Technique**
Ad Agency: **Blunt Hann Sersen, Inc.**
Client: **Davis and Geck**
Art Director: **Tony Barone**
Illustrator: **Leonard Dank**
Copywriter: **Jean Allan**

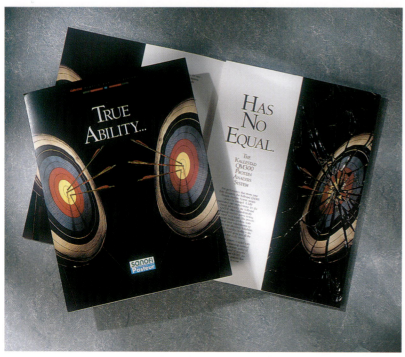

Product: **QM300**
Title of Graphic: **QM300 Brochure**
Ad Agency: **Nanos & Gray, Inc.**
Client: **Sanofi Diagnostics Pasteur**
Art Director: **Dawn Allman**
Photographer: **Marc McCabe**
Copywriter: **Linda Salvay**

Sales Promotion

Product: **Nasalcrom**
Title of Graphic: **You Don't Have to Run and Hide**
Ad Agency: **Sandler Communications**
Client: **Fisons Pharmaceuticals**
Art Director: **Lori Mulhern**
Illustrator: **Frank Bolle**
Copywriter: **Lisa Stec**

Product: **Nasalcrom**
Title of Graphic: **Block Allergy Symptoms Before They Become Monumental**
Ad Agency: **Sandler Communications**
Client: **Fisons Pharmaceuticals**
Art Director: **Lori Mulhern**
Illustrator: **Mark Summers**
Copywriter: **Lisa Stec**

Sales Promotion

Product: **SR1**
Title of Graphic: **Logo**
Design Firm: **Lewis & Gace, Inc.**
Client: **Serono-Baker Diagnostics**
Art Director: **Rose Farber**
Illustrator: **Rose Farber**

Sales Promotion

Because Time Is of the Essence in Assessing and Treating the Infertile Couple

It's estimated that upwards of 20% of all American couples experience some type of fertility problem. This incidence is rising with the increase in sexually transmitted disease. The road to helping the infertile couple achieve and maintain a pregnancy begins with appropriate hormonal assessment. For the busy physician and the anxious couple...*time is of the essence.*

Optimal Evaluation Requires a Variety of Assays Performed in a Timely Manner

A complete hormonal "workup" includes assays of estradiol, FSH, hCG, LH, progesterone, prolactin, and thyroid levels. The timing of these assays is also critical. For example, determination of estradiol, FSH, and LH levels, on Day 9 of the menstrual cycle, can help differentiate the hormonally normal female from one suffering hypothalamic hypogonadotropism, premature menopause, or polycystic ovarian disease. Determination of the estradiol level on Day 13, in conjunction with ultrasound evaluation, can help the physician choose the appropriate pharmacotherapy to either induce ovulation or continue follicular stimulation.

To identify the underlying cause of infertility, select the optimal pharmacologic regimen, or properly time IVF or GIFT procedures, a complete hormonal workup performed in a timely manner is essential.

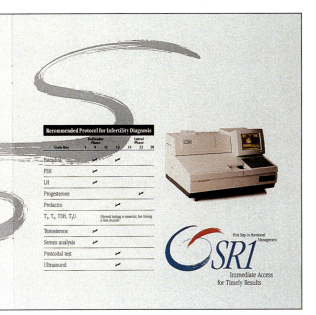

Recommended Protocol for Infertility Diagnosis

Cycle Day	Follicular Phase			Luteal Phase	
	1	9	11	13	14	22	28
Estradiol		✓		✓			
FSH		✓					
LH		✓					
Progesterone						✓	
Prolactin							
T_3, T_4, TSH, T_3U	(thyroid testing is essential, but timing is less crucial)
Testosterone	✓						
Semen analysis	✓						
Postcoital test					✓		
Ultrasound					✓		

SR1 — First Step in Hormonal Management
Immediate Access for Timely Results

Because Time Is of the Essence SR1 Combines Simple, Walk-Away Operation...

The SR1 offers you the simplest operation procedure of any immunoassay system available. Its unique cartridge system provides automatic pipetting, mixing, incubation, measurement, and reporting of results. The operator simply adds the patient sample to the cartridge and places the cartridge on the SR1 loading ramp. Reporting of results, even simultaneous multiple batches, begins in approximately an hour. The bar code wand automatically enters assay type and unique I.D. so there is never a question that the patient is correctly matched to the result. Even the waste disposal is self-contained, minimizing operator contact with body fluids. And because it is non-isotopic technology, there is no concern about radioactivity and its associated risks and expense.

With the Flexibility Your Busy Practice Requires

SR1 is ready when you are, providing 24-hour-a-day, 7-day-a-week testing capability. The automated immediate access capability allows immediate repeat performance of abnormal values and provides immediate availability for STATs. Sequential batch testing allows testing for the same assay or simultaneous assaying of different test batches. And, because SR1 software provides a simple means of system update, you'll always have the most advanced immunoassay system available. On time, in no time.

- **A** quiet printer
- **B** user-friendly on-screen instructions
- **C** upgradable software discs
- **D** sealed keypad
- **E** bar code wand
- **F** temperature-controlled carousel
- **G** easily accessible common reagents
- **H** convenient cartridge loading ramp
- **I** disposable waste container

- Fully automated operation:
  - automatically measures and mixes reagents
  - controls timing and temperature for test cartridges
  - reads, analyzes, and reports results
- Automated immediate access capability:
  - performs profiles and panels
  - allows immediate repeat performance of abnormal values
  - provides instant availability for STATs
- Operator-controlled on-line dilution
- Sequential batching capability performs multiple batches simultaneously

- Comprehensive assay menu will include:
  - reproductive hormones
  - thyroid hormones
  - infectious disease markers
  - therapeutic drugs
  - nutritional assessment
- Bar code labeling matches patients with results
- Custom patient reporting provides demographics and profiles
- 80-sample capacity for large runs and continuous access
- Compact, bench-top design
- At a price that suits your budget

SR1 — First Step in Hormonal Management
Immediate Access for Timely Results

Consider What SR1 Can Do for Your Patients and for You...

Competitively priced SR1 offers you and your patients unique benefits over reliance on an outside source or alternate immunoassay system. SR1 provides the simplest operation available, and can put results in your hands in approximately one hour... possibly before the patient leaves your office. SR1 can help you optimize the diagnosis of infertility problems and make more timely treatment decisions, while helping to reduce patient anxiety and stress.

...Because Time Is Money

- SR1 lets you control the rising cost of infertility management
- More cost efficient than sending tests out or using a different immunoassay system
- Simple walk-away operation can be learned easily by any member of your staff
- Saves time and reduces labor costs – frees staff from time-consuming phone calls to track down results

- Provides the flexibility to perform profiles, simultaneous batches or STAT testing
- Eliminates the expense of radioactive waste disposal
- Equips your office with "referral center" capacities

"My SR1 increased my nurse's efficiency significantly...saves us the time she used to spend phoning labs, and logging test results."

"My SR1 gives me a powerful diagnostic advantage: immunoassay results while my patient is still in the office."

Yes! Time Is of the Essence

And Time Is Money!

☐ Please arrange an SR1 Customized Cost/Profit Analysis.
☐ Have a representative contact me.
☐ I would like a video demonstration.
☐ Send additional information on SR1 Immunoassay System.

Name
Office phone   Best time to call   AM   PM
Address
City   State   Zip Code

Learn How SR1 Can Save You Time... And Money

To see how affordable and profitable SR1 can be in your practice, arrange an SR1 Customized Cost/Profit Analysis. Simply call 1-800-345-3127, or contact your Serono-Baker Diagnostics representative. If you prefer, complete and return the attached reply card. But please do it today, because time really is money!

SR1 — First Step in Hormonal Management
Immediate Access for Timely Results

Sales Promotion

Product: **Eucerin Daily Facial Lotion**
Title of Graphic: **Face Introduction Box Mailer**
Ad Agency: **Hall Decker McKibbin, Inc.**
Client: **Beiersdorf, Inc.**
Art Director: **Doreen Sabatino**
Illustrator: **Lori Anzalone**
Copywriter: **Wendy Friedman**
Structural Designer: **Packaging Trends**

Product: **Isoptin SR**
Title of Graphic: **Heart-in-Harmony Program**
Ad Agency: **Blunt Hann Sersen, Inc.**
Client: **Knoll Pharmaceuticals**
Art Director: **Jeff Lipman**
Illustrator: **Jim Hedden**
Copywriter: **Jean Allan**
Structural Designer: **Howell Packaging**

Sales Promotion

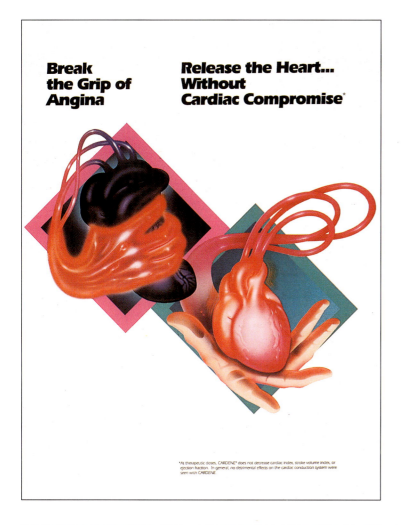

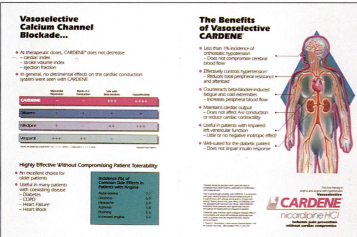

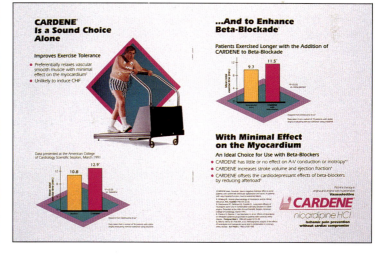

Product: **Cardene**
Title of Graphic: **Sales Aid**
Ad Agency: **Lewis & Gace, Inc.**
Client: **Syntex Laboratories**
Art Director: **Warren McLeod/Glynnis Osher**
Illustrator: **Gerd Dagne**
Photographer: **Tom Arma**
Copywriter: **Barbara Goldschmidt**

Sales Promotion

Product: **Dipentum**
Title of Graphic: **The First Oral Delivery**
Ad Agency: **Blunt Hann Sersen, Inc.**
Client: **Kabi Pharmacia, Inc.**
Art Director: **Don Sersen**
Illustrator: **Ron Lotozo**
Copywriter: **Karen Blunt**

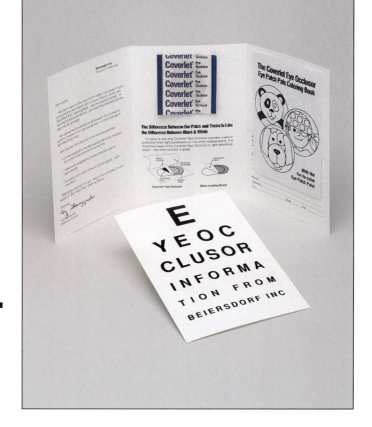

Product: **Coverlet Eye Occlusor**
Title of Graphic: **Eye Chart**
Ad Agency: **Hall Decker McKibbin, Inc.**
Client: **Beiersdorf, Inc.**
Art Director: **Doreen Sabatino**
Photographer: **Russ Avarella**
Copywriter: **Karen Stoia**

Sales Promotion

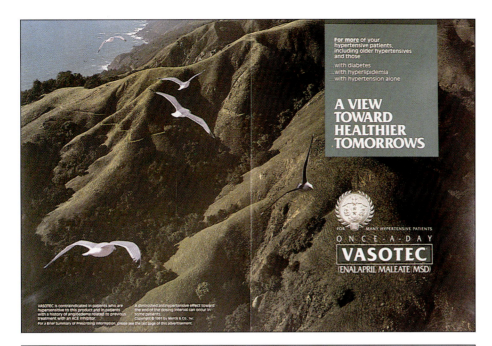

Product: **Vasotec**
Ad Agency: **Vicom/FCB**
Client: **Merck, Sharpe & Dohme**
Art Director: **Julie Kenly**
Photographer: **Richard H. Smith**
Copywriter: **Liz Hevey**

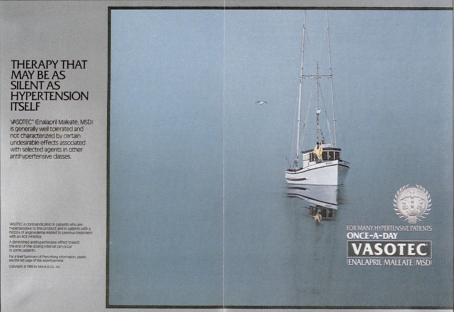

Product: **Vasotec**
Title of Graphic: **Boat Insert**
Ad Agency: **Vicom/FCB**
Client: **Merck, Sharpe & Dohme**
Art Director: **Julie Kenly**
Photographer: **Richard H. Smith**
Copywriter: **Liz Hevey**

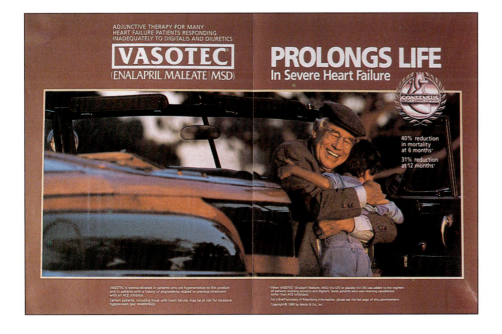

Product: **Vasotec**
Title of Graphic: **Consensus Journal Insert**
Ad Agency: **Vicom/FCB**
Client: **Merck, Sharpe & Dohme**
Art Director: **Julie Kenly**
Photographer: **David Burnett**
Copywriter: **Liz Hevey**

Sales Promotion

Product: **Prinzide**
Title of Graphic: **Guru, Submarine, Parachute**
Ad Agency: **Vicom/FCB**
Client: **Merck, Sharp & Dohme**
Art Director: **Maryanna Zamiska/Peter M. Plante (MSD)**
Illustrator: **Tom Payne**
Copywriter: **Robert Krell**

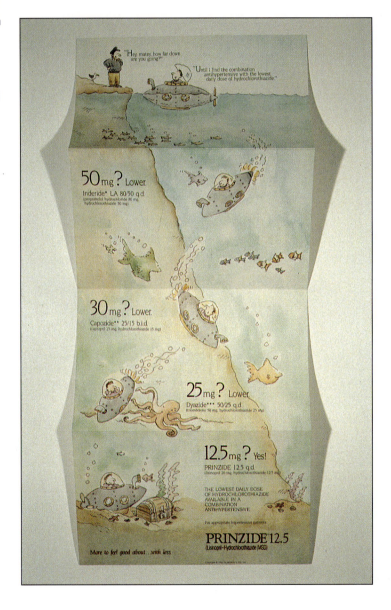

Sales Promotion

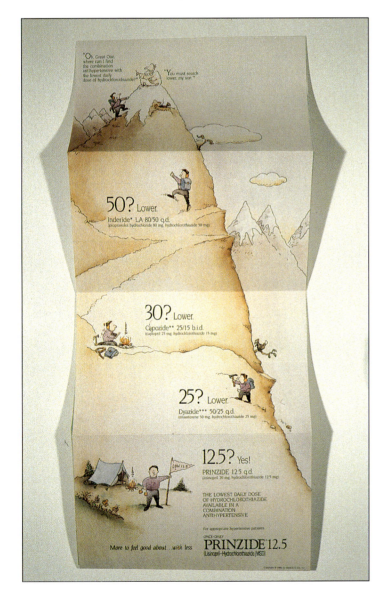

Sales Promotion

Product: **Ergamisol**
Title of Graphic: **Standards of the Twentieth Century**
Ad Agency: **Botto, Roessner, Horne & Messinger**
Client: **Janssen Phamaceutica**
Art Director: **Aram Chenensky**
Illustrator: **Adam Niklewicz, Time Alt, Michael Morenko**
Copywriter: **Cathy Popescu**

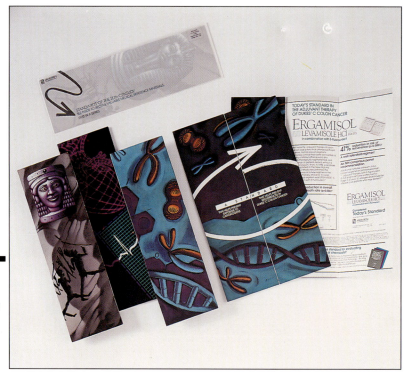

Product: **Rogaine (minoxidil 2%)**
Title of Graphic: **Common Hereditary Hair Loss: What Happens to Your Hair and How Rogaine Topical Solution can Help**
Design Firm: **MedPro Communications, Inc.**
Client: **The Upjohn Company**
Art Director: **Catherine Twomey**
Illustrator: **Catherine Twomey**
Copywriter: **Diane Dreher**

Common Hereditary Hair Loss: What Happens To Your Hair And How Rogaine® Topical Solution (minoxidil 2%) Can Help

Common hereditary hair loss is the most common form of hair loss in men and women. This type of hair loss typically begins in the teens, twenties, or thirties.

Common hereditary hair loss is known by a variety of names, including *male pattern baldness*, *androgenetic alopecia*, and *female diffuse alopecia*. In medical terms hair loss is called *alopecia*. The medical term *androgenetic* describes the cause of the hair loss. *Andro* indicates that the hair loss is related to the production of male hormones called androgens, which can affect hair growth. The term *genetic* indicates that the condition is inherited.

In males, the characteristic patterns of hereditary hair loss vary widely. Some men just show exaggerated recession of the frontal hairline, while others may lose all of their hair except the fringe around the sides. Most balding men fall somewhere between these extremes (Figure 1).

What we commonly know as the "hair" is actually only the *visible* portion of the hair, called the *hair shaft*. Each hair shaft arises from a pouchlike structure below the skin called a *follicle*. As hair grows, dies, and falls out, the follicle repeatedly goes through three stages from active to inactive. When active, hair follicles are long and deeply embedded under the skin (Figure 2).

All hair follicles have the same structure and go through the same repeated cycles of active growth and rest. We are born with all of our hair follicles. No new ones will develop after birth.

The growth cycle is much like an on-off system consisting of three stages or phases: anagen, catagen, and telogen.

Anagen, the growing phase, lasts approximately 1,000 days in humans, but it can range from 2 to 6 years. During anagen, the thickness of the hair shaft increases, and the hair reaches maximum length (Figure 3).

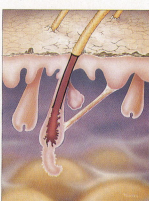

Figure 4. Catagen.

Catagen, the transitional phase, signals the end of the growth phase. It is very short, lasting from 1 to 2 weeks. During catagen, the follicle rapidly decreases in volume, and the lower part of the follicle is destroyed (Figure 4).

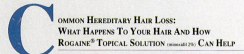

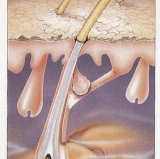

Figure 3. Anagen.

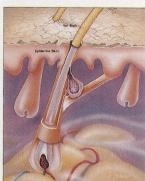

Figure 2. Hair follicle.

Figure 1. Patterns of hair loss.

© 1990 The Upjohn Company

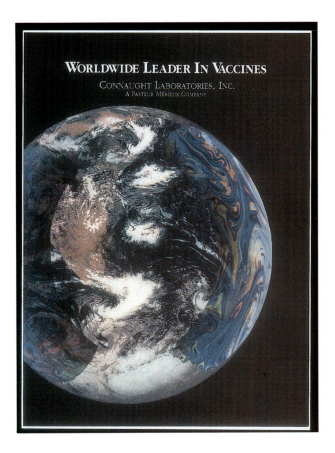

Title of Graphic: **Chemotherapy-Induced Emesis**
Ad Agency: **Barnum & Souza, Inc.**
Client: **U.S. Pharmacist Cover Contest**
Art Director: **Eric Marcus**
Photographer: **Nick Koudis**

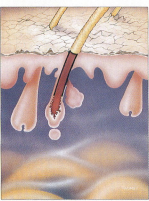

Figure 5. Telogen.

Telogen, the resting phase of the cycle, lasts 5 to 6 weeks. The follicle is inactive at this time, during which a new hair forms. The telogen follicle is short, approximately one half to one third of the length of a growing follicle (Figure 5).

After telogen, activity in the hair follicle is renewed, signifying **a return to the anagen** phase. A new hair shaft forms and grows alongside the old hair, forcing the old hair to fall out (Figure 6).

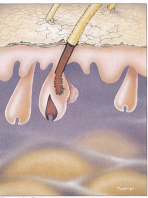

Figure 6. Return to anagen.

Hair follicles are not synchronized; each one goes through these phases independently. At any given time, approximately 90% of the follicles are in the growing phase, and 10% are resting. On average, we normally lose up to 100 resting hairs each day, and approximately the same number of follicles enter the growing phase.

Normally, as the hair cycles through these phases, follicles tend to return to the same length and size during anagen. In common hereditary hair loss, certain follicles become gradually smaller, or *miniaturized*, over time. The number of follicles

Figure 7. Miniaturization of the follicle.

that become miniaturized depends on the heredity of the person. As the follicles become smaller, they produce smaller, finer hairs with each growth cycle (Figure 7). Eventually, this can result in short, thin, light hairs that are barely visible above the scalp surface.

Because the follicles are still present, it is possible to reverse the miniaturization process and cause the affected follicles to enlarge again.

ROGAINE Topical Solution (minoxidil 2%) Can Reverse Follicle Miniaturization
ROGAINE Topical Solution is the only proven treatment for androgenetic alopecia. Under the influence of ROGAINE, miniaturized hair follicles become partially enlarged, producing longer, coarser, darker hairs (Figure 8). These hairs cover the scalp to a greater extent than does the hair from miniaturized follicles.

It is important to use ROGAINE correctly and to have realistic expectations about the treatment before you begin. While no individual response to ROGAINE can be predicted in advance, clinical studies indicate that some men tend to respond better than others. The more miniaturized follicles remaining in the affected area, the more likely that there will be a response to ROGAINE. Thus, men who have been losing hair for a short time are likely to respond better than those who have been affected for long periods. Men with smaller scalp areas affected by hair loss are likely to respond better than men with more extensive hair loss. In general, a younger patient is

Figure 8. Miniaturization reversed with ROGAINE

more likely to respond than an older patient. Though these factors provide some indication of response, they are not absolute. Trial treatment is the only method to determine response in an individual. Ask your doctor about treatment with ROGAINE.

Sales Promotion

Product: **Benadryl Decongestant Elixir**
Title of Graphic: **Diminish Winter Cold Symptoms with One Word . . .**
Ad Agency: **Sudler & Hennessey**
Client: **Parke-Davis Consumer Health Products Group**
Art Director: **Meg Levine/Siu Yuen Chan**
Illustrator: **Pam Wall**
Photographer: **Shel Secunda**
Copywriter: **Sandra Holtzman**

Product: **Ohmeda MRI**
Title of Graphic: **MRI Promotion**
Ad Agency: **Rosner & Rubin, Inc.**
Client: **Ohmeda**
Art Director: **Gene Rosner**
Photogrpaher: **Ron Seymour**
Copywriter: **Todd VanSlyke**

Sales Promotion

Product: **Voltaren**
Title of Graphic: **3-D Mailing Box**
Ad Agency: **Salthouse Torre Norton, Inc.**
Client: **Ciba-Geigy Pharmaceutical**
Art Director: **Mike Lazar/Juan Ramos**
Illustrator: **Clockwork Apple**
Photographer: **Carmine Macedonia**
Copywriter: **Peter Chamedes**
Structural Designer: **Trimensions, Inc.**

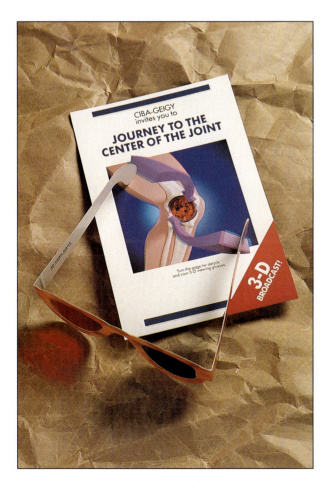

Product: **Voltaren**
Title of Graphic: **Liftime Guide Backcover**
Ad Agency: **Salthouse Torre Norton, Inc.**
Client: **Ciba-Geigy Pharmaceutical**
Art Director: **Mike Lazur/Juan Ramos**
Photographer: **Carmine Macedonia**
Copywriter: **Peter Chamedes**
Structural Designer: **Clockwork Apple**

Sales Promotion

Product: **Mevacor**
Title of Graphic: **Cholesterol Reduction Wheel**
Ad Agency: **Hal Lewis Group**
Client: **Merck Sharp & Dohme, International**
Art Director: **Dave Winigrad**
Photographer: **Asterisk, Inc.**
Copywriter: **Alan Rubin**
Structural Designer: **Graphic Calculator Co.**

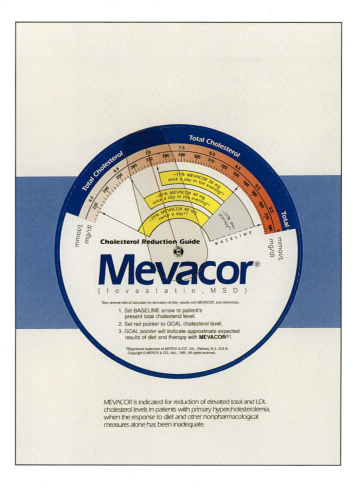

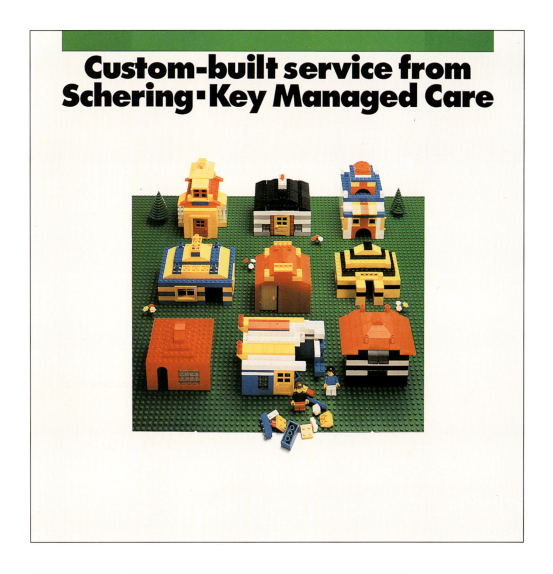

Product: **Entire Product Line**
Title of Graphic: **Custom-Built Service from Schering/Key Managed Care**
Ad Agency: **William Douglas McAdams, Inc.**
Client: **Schering/Key Managed Care**
Art Director: **Haig Adishian**
Photographer: **Murray Shear/Paul Frankian**
Copywriter: **Gwenne Frieman**
Structural Designer: **Structural Graphics**

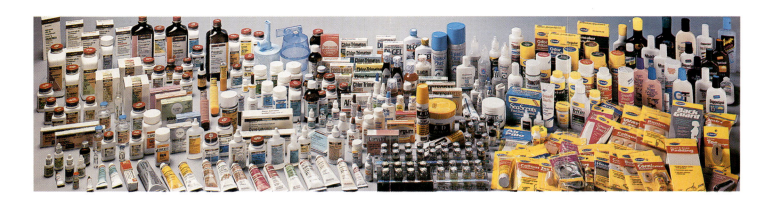

Sales Promotion

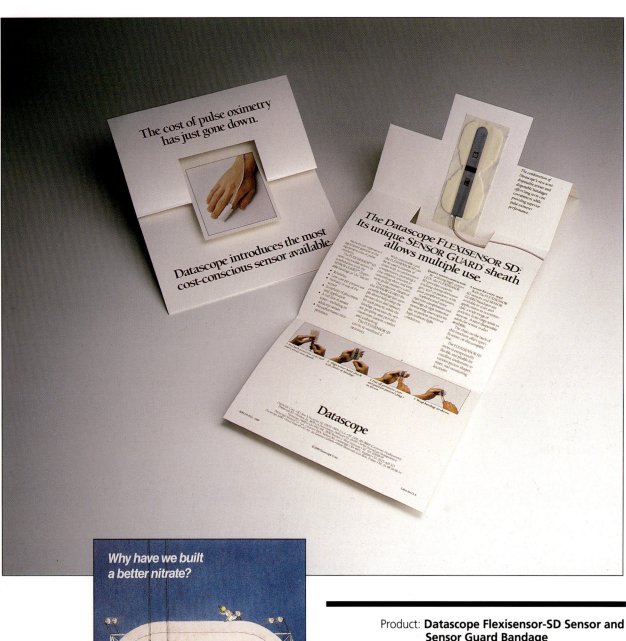

Product: **Datascope Flexisensor-SD Sensor and Sensor Guard Bandage**
Title of Graphic: **Flexisensor/Sensor Guard Promo Aid**
Ad Agency: **Dick Jackson, Inc.**
Client: **Datascope Corp.**
Art Director: **David Lukshus**
Photographer: **Ralph Massullo**
Copywriter: **Richard Jackson**
Structural Designer: **Structural Graphics, Inc.**

Product: **Transderm-Nitro**
Title of Graphic: **Transderm-Nitro Sales Aid**
Ad Agency: **C & G Advertising Agency, Inc.**
Client: **Ciba-Geigy Pharmaceuticals**
Art Director: **John Hovell**
Illustrator: **Al Lorenz**
Copywriter: **Deanne Napurano**

Sales Promotion

Product: **Transderm-Nitro**
Title of Graphic: **All Nitrates are not Created Equal**
Ad Agency: **C & G Advertising Agency, Inc.**
Client: **Ciba-Geigy Pharmaceuticals**
Art Director: **Ron Vareltzis**
Illustrator: **Steve Hieman**
Photographer: **Ed Gallucci**
Copywriter: **Deanne Napurano**

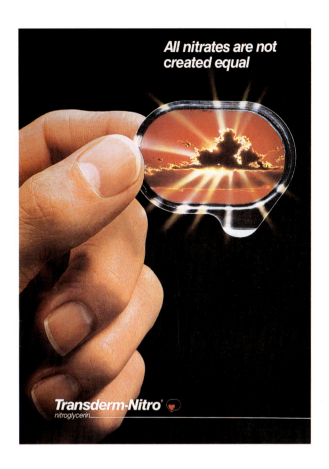

Product: **Actigall**
Title of Graphic: **When Your Patients Complain of Chronic Abdominal Distress**
Ad Agency: **C & G Advertising Agency, Inc.**
Client: **Summit Pharmaceuticals**
Art Director: **Robert Talarczyk**
Illustrator: **Gretchen Place**
Copywriter: **Karen Neale**

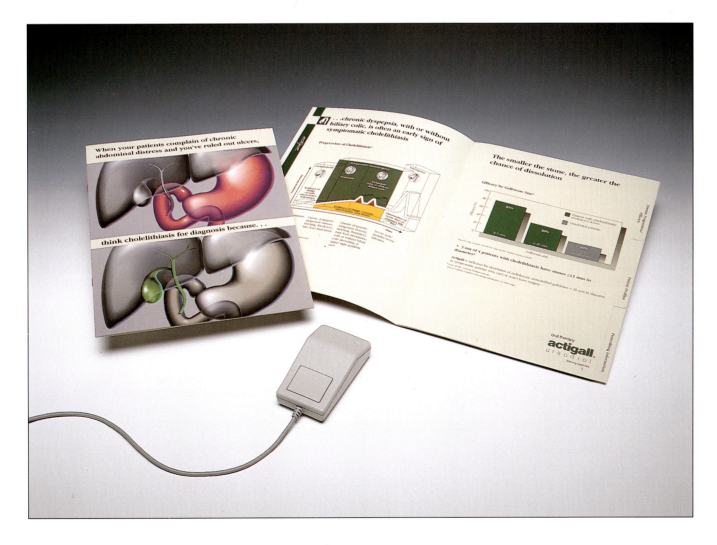

Sales Promotion

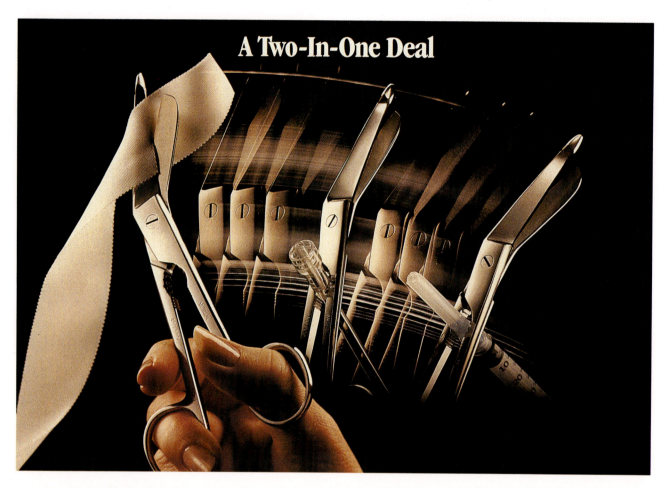

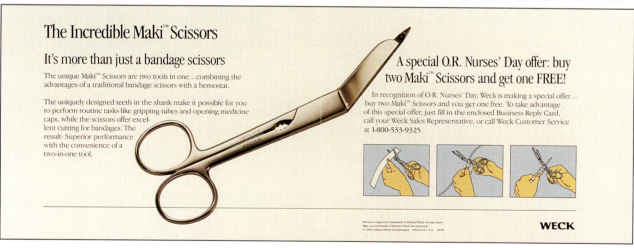

Product: **Maki Scissors**
Title of Graphic: **3 in 1 Deal**
Ad Agency: **Simms & McIvor Marketing Communications**
Client: **Weck Instruments**
Art Director: **Francine Martin**
Illustrator: **Art Kretzschmar**
Photographer: **Neil Molinaro**
Copywriter: **Renee Fustos**

Sales Promotion

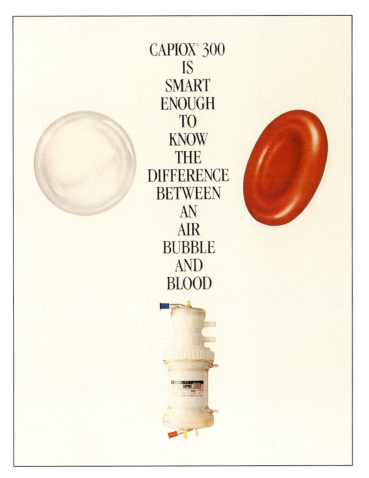

Product: **Capiox 300 Series Oxygenator**
Title of Graphic: **Blood & Bubbles**
Ad Agency: **Simms & McIvor Marketing Communications**
Client: **Terumo Corp.**
Art Director: **Francine Martin**
Illustrator: **Art Kretzschme**
Photographer: **Kevin Black**
Copywriter: **Dick Ahnert**

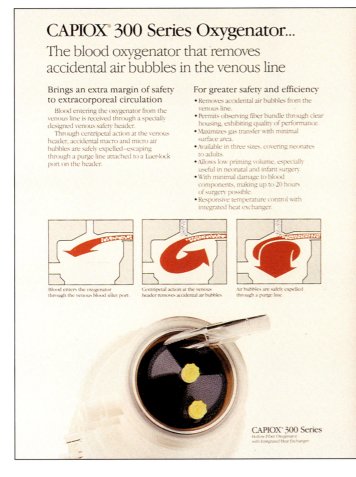
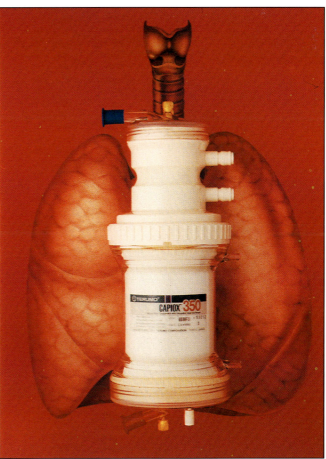

Sales Promotion

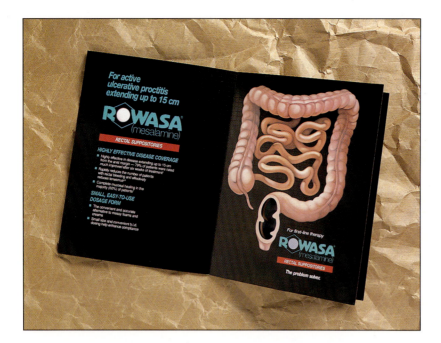

Product: **Rowasa**
Title of Graphic: **Covered**
Ad Agency: **Salthouse Torre Norton, Inc.**
Client: **Solvay Pharmaceutical**
Art Director: **David Recchia**
Illustrator: **Lou Bory**
Copywriter: **Peter Chamedes**

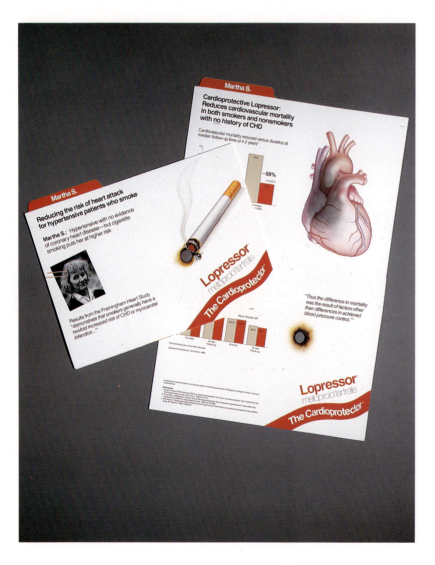

Product: **Lopressor**
Title of Graphic: **Cigarette Burn**
Ad Agency: **C & G Advertising Agency, Inc.**
Client: **Ciba-Geigy Pharmaceuticals**
Art Director: **Myrtle Johnson**
Illustrator: **Steve Martin/Bob Demarest**
Copywriter: **Kevin Purcell/Karen Neale**

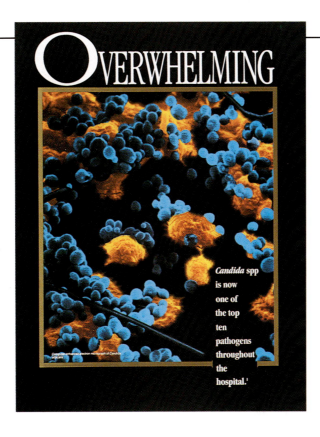

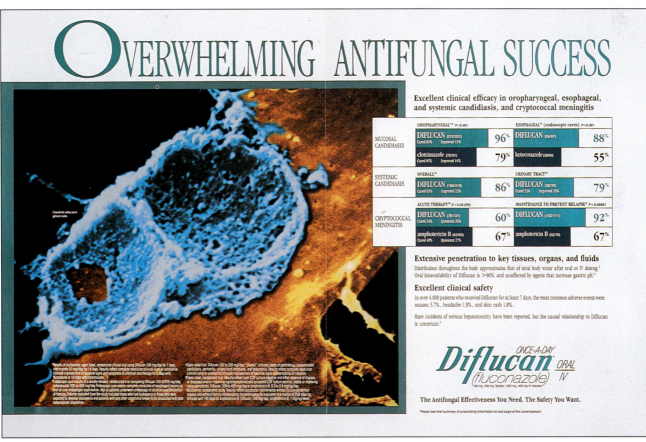

Product: **Diflucan**
Title of Graphic: **Overwhelming**
Ad Agency: **Cline, Davis & Mann, Inc.**
Client: **Roerig**
Art Director: **Janet Rappaport**
Copywriter: **Ed Wise**

Sales Promotion

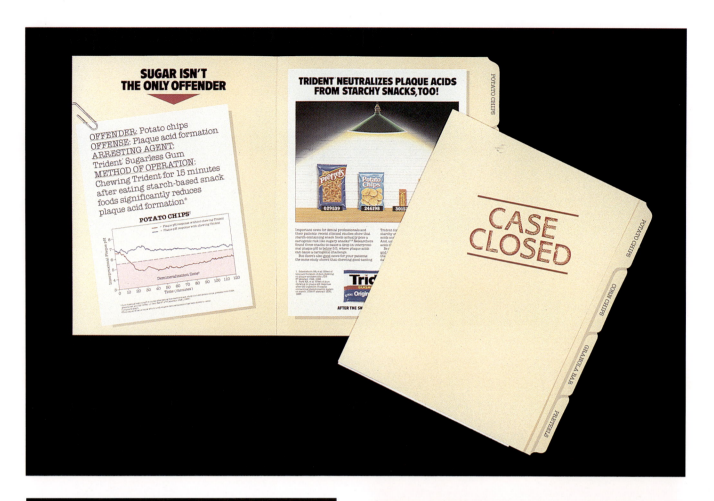

Product: **Trident**
Title of Graphic: **Case Closed**
Ad Agency: **Thomas G. Ferguson Associates, Inc.**
Client: **Warner Lambert Company, Inc.**
Art Director: **Mike Fiore**
Illustrator: **Bill Devlin**
Copywriter: **Paula Sciarrino**

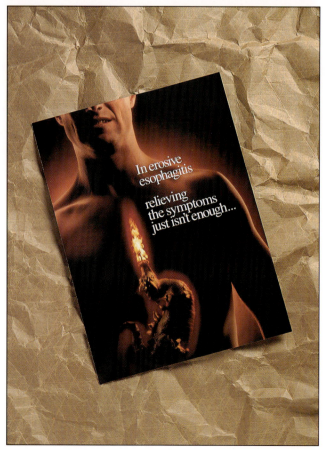

Product: **Tagemet**
Title of Graphic: **Relieving the Symptoms Just isn't Enough**
Ad Agency: **Salthouse Torre Norton, Inc.**
Client: **SmithKline Beecham Pharmaceutical**
Art Director: **William C. Beauchamp**
Photographer: **Neil Molinaro**
Copywriter: **Chuck Dexter**

Sales Promotion

Product: **Delta-Lite FlashCast**
Title of Graphic: **FlashCast Sales Aid**
Ad Agency: **Gerbig Snell/Weisheimer & Associates**
Client: **Johnson & Johnson Orthopaedics**
Art Director: **Diane Hay**
Photographer: **Morton & White**
Copywriter: **Elizabeth Ficocelli**

Sales Promotion

Product: **Norgesic Forte**
Title of Graphic: **Working Together**
Ad Agency: **Girgenti, Hughes, Butler & McDowell**
Client: **3M Pharmaceuticals**
Art Director: **Mark McDowell**
Photographer: **Marc David Cohen**
Copywriter: **Bob Ranieri**

Title of Graphic: **We Succeed Where Others Fail**
Ad Agency: **Girgenti, Hughes, Butler & McDowell**
Client: **Medtronic**
Art Director: **Scott Frank**
Photographer: **Chip Forelli**
Copywriter: **Frank Hughes**

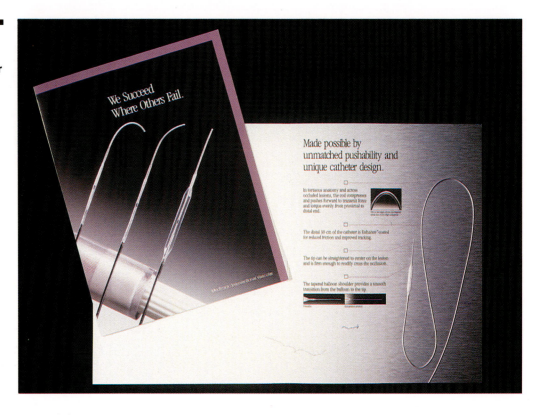

Sales Promotion

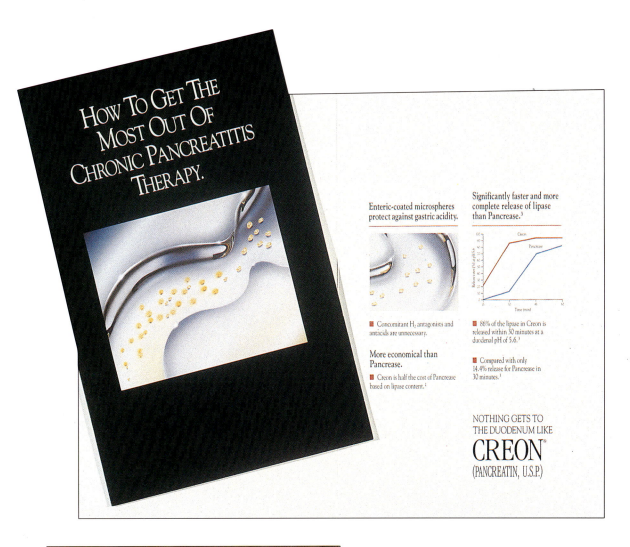

Product: **Creon**
Title of Graphic: **How to Get the Most . . .**
Ad Agency: **Girgenti, Hughes, Butler & McDowell**
Client: **Solvay**
Art Director: **Mark McDowell**
Illustrator: **Jeff Holewski**
Copywriter: **Frank Hughes**

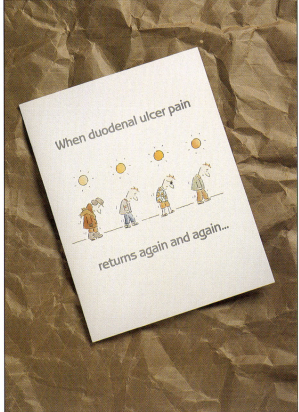

Product: **Tagamet**
Title of Graphic: **When Duodenal Ulcer Pain . . .**
Ad Agency: **Salthouse Torre Norton, Inc.**
Client: **SmithKline Beecham Pharmaceutical**
Art Director: **Gail Berlese**
Illustrator: **Alex Tiani**
Copywriter: **Chuck Dexter**

Sales Promotion

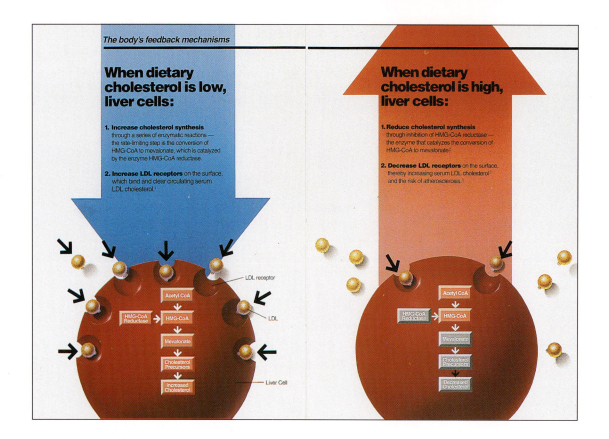

Product: **Zocor**
Title of Graphic: **Mechanism of Action Detail**
Ad Agency: **The Hal Lewis Group**
Client: **Merck, Sharp & Dohme**
Art Director: **David Winigrad**
Illustrator: **Keith Kasnot**
Copywriter: **Alan Rubin**

Sales Promotion

Product: **Heartgard-30**
Title of Graphic: **Heartworm Prevention**
Ad Agency: **Warhaftig Associates, Inc.**
Client: **MSD Agvet, Division of Merck & Co., Inc.**
Art Director: **Matt Warhaftig, Mary Cunningham**
Photographer: **J&M Studio, Landmark, Kent/Donna Dannen**
Copywriter: **Jonathan Hughes**

Product: **Engerix-B**
Title of Graphic: **Profiles in Risk: The Healthcare Worker**
Ad Agency: **Salthouse Torre Norton, Inc.**
Client: **SmithKline Beecham Pharmaceutical**
Art Director: **Neil Paulino**
Illustrator: **Terry Hoff**
Copywriter: **Marlene Molinoff**

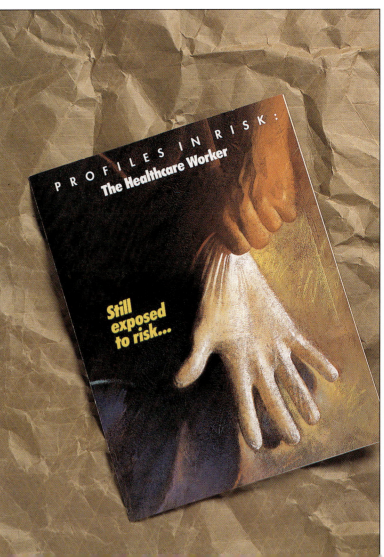

Product: **Pancrease MT**
Title of Graphic: **Cystic Fibrosis Currents Special Edition**
Ad Agency: **Botto, Roessner, Horne & Messinger**
Client: **McNeil Pharmaceutical**
Art Director: **Aram Chenensky**
Copywriter: **Suzanne Shubart**

Sales Promotion

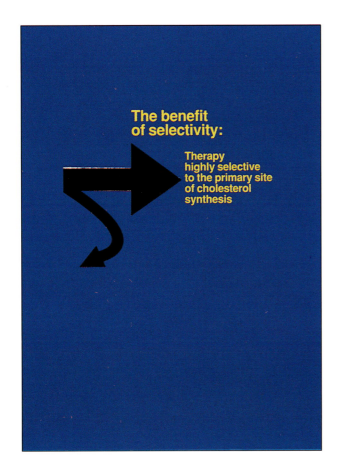

Product: **Mevacor**
Title of Graphic: **July 91 Detail Aid**
Ad Agency: **Gross Townsend Frank Hoffman**
Client: **Merck, Sharp & Dohme**
Art Director: **Monica Garb**
Copywriter: **Bebe Barbour**

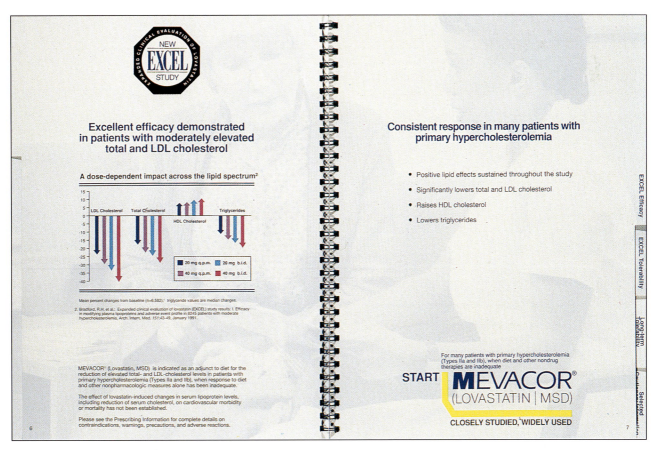

Sales Promotion

Product: **Theracys BCG Live (intravesical)**
Title of Graphic: **Transureathral Resection of the Bladder**
Ad Agency: **Medical Art, Inc.**
Art Director: **Judith Glick**
Illustrator: **Judith Glick**

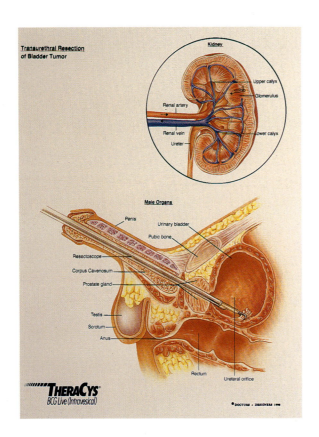
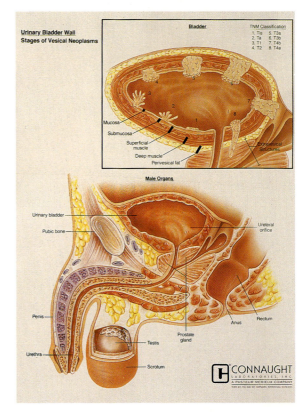

Product: **Synarel**
Title of Graphic: **Understanding Endometriosis Patient Aid**
Ad Agency: **Baxter, Gurian and Mazzei, Inc.**
Client: **Syntex**
Art Director: **Art Nagano**
Illustrator: **Cynthia Turner**
Copywriter: **Nancy Richard**

Sales Promotion

Product: **Proventil**
Title of Graphic: **It's All in the Family**
Ad Agency: **Klemtner Advertising**
Client: **Schering Corp.**
Art Director: **Elizabeth Elfenbein**
Copywriter: **Melissa de Fiebere**
Structural Designer: **Trimensions, Inc.**

Sales Promotion

Ad Agency: **Vicom/FCB**
Client: **Syntex**
Art Director: **Jerry Malone**
Photographer: **Comstock**
Copywriter: **Larry Septoff/Bob Finkel**

Sales Promotion

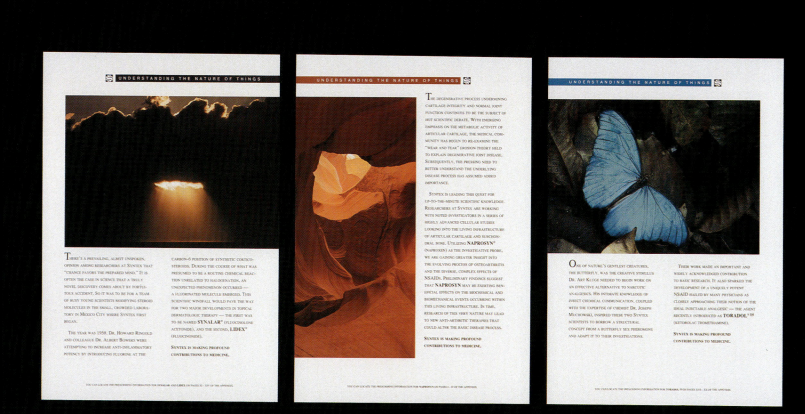

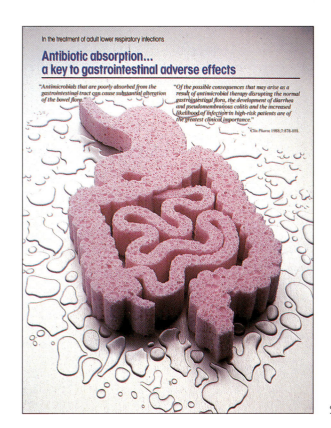

Product: **Ceclor**
Title of Graphic: **Antibiotic Absorption**
Ad Agency: **J. Walter Thompson Healthcare**
Client: **Eli Lilly and Company**
Art Director: **Steven Frederick**
Photographer: **Richard Levy**
Copywriter: **Mary Schimpf**
Structural Designer: **Manhattan Model Makers**

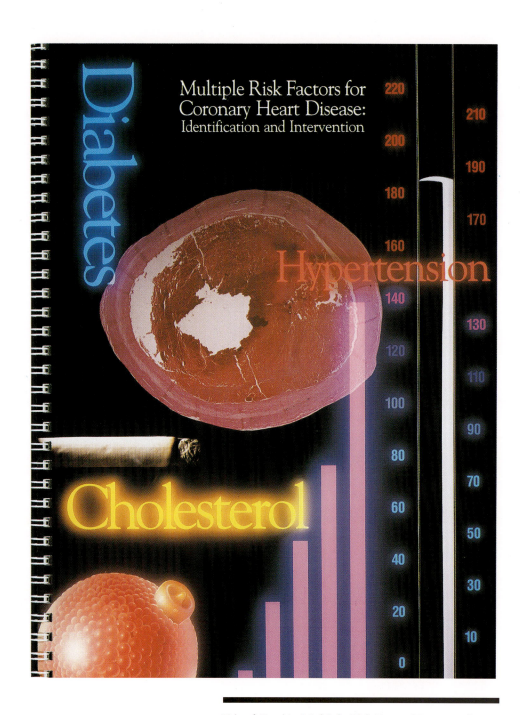

Title of Graphic: **Multiple Risk Factor Monograph**
Ad Agency: **The Hal Lewis Group**
Client: **Merck, Sharp & Dohme International**
Art Director: **David Winigrad**
Illustrator: **Rich D'Ginto**
Photographer: **Asterisk, Inc.**
Copywriter: **Alan Rubin**

Sales Promotion

Case History #3

SEX: Female
AGE: 56
RISK FACTORS:
- No family history of CHD
- Mild hypertension (systolic blood pressure–140 mmHg)
- Normal weight
- Smoker
- Total cholesterol–240 mg/dl
- HDL cholesterol–60 mg/dl

RECOMMENDATION: Diet therapy/smoking cessation

Modifiable Risk Factors

> Cholesterol, blood pressure, and smoking are among the risk factors that the practicing physician can treat.

Modifiable risk factors include cholesterol level, blood pressure, and smoking. Identifying and modifying these risk factors may improve and prolong life.

CHOLESTEROL

Lipoproteins are composed of two layers: an outer, water-soluble layer, consisting primarily of apolipoproteins, phospholipids, and free cholesterol, and a core containing cholesterol esters and triglyceride.

Lipoproteins originate in the gut as chylomicrons. They progressively decrease in size, changing composition as they evolve from chylomicrons to very-low-density lipoproteins (VLDL), to intermediate-density lipoproteins (IDL), to low-density lipoproteins (LDL), and, finally, to high-density lipoproteins (HDL).

> A large volume of compelling evidence links elevated serum cholesterol to CHD worldwide.

A large volume of compelling evidence links elevated serum cholesterol to CHD worldwide. Among the most important longitudinal studies are the Framingham Study, the Whitehall study of civil servants in London, the British Regional Heart Study, the Oslo Study, and the Multiple Risk Factor Intervention Trial (MRFIT). Findings from these studies have been supported by results from intervention trials such as the Oslo Diet and Smoking Trial, Lipids Research Clinics Coronary Primary Prevention Trial (LRC-CPPT), and the Helsinki Heart Study showing that the incidence of CHD is reduced when cholesterol levels are lowered.

CHOLESTEROL AND CHD MORTALITY

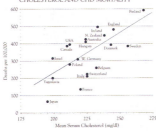

Coronary heart disease mortality rate versus serum cholesterol.
(Adapted, with permission, from Simons LA *Am J Cardiol* 57:5G, 1986)

DIAGRAMMATIC REPRESENTATION OF LIPOPROTEIN STRUCTURE

- Phospholipid
- Free Cholesterol
- Triglyceride
- Cholesterol Ester

LIPOPROTEINS AND HYPERLIPIDEMIA

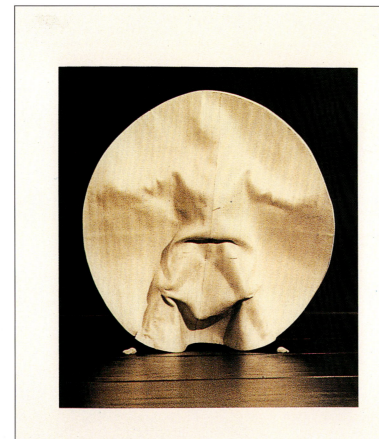

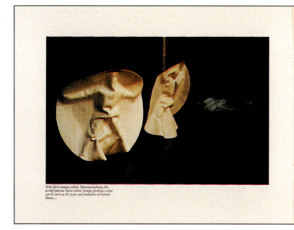

Title of Graphic: **Menninger Capabilities Brochure**
Ad Agency: **Esprit Communications, Inc.**
Client: **Mills-Peninsula Hospitals**
Art Director: **Robert Bogart**
Photographer: **Michel Buhrer**
Copywriter: **Peter Jacoby**

Sales Promotion

Title of Graphic: **Tough Choices Ad**
Ad Agency: **Esprit Communications, Inc.**
Client: **Caremark**
Art Director: **Robert Bogart**
Photographer: **Bill Sumner**
Copywriter: **Peter Jacoby**

Title of Graphic: **Imagyn Corporate Identity**
Ad Agency: **Esprit Communications, Inc.**
Client: **Imagyn Medical, Inc.**
Art Director: **Robert Bogart**
Copywriter: **Peter Jacoby**

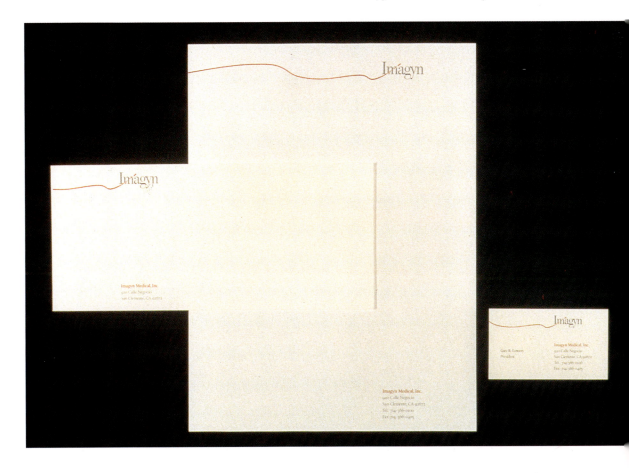

Sales Promotion

Title of Graphic: **The Ellice and Rosa McDonald Fund**
Design Firm: **Art as Applied to Medicine/Johns Hopkins**
Client: **Facial Prosthetics Clinic/Art as Applied To Medicine/Johns Hopkins**
Art Director: **Joseph M. Dieter, Jr.**
Copywriter: **Department Staff**

Product: **Cardiac Assist Devices (ICS 8000, BVS 5000, Artificial Heart)**
Title of Graphic: **Corporate Image Brochure**
Ad Agency: **Grob & Co., Inc.**
Client: **Abiomed Cardiovascular, Inc.**
Art Director: **Breda Kenyon**
Illustrator: **Andrea Thayer**
Photographer: **Michael Weymouth Design**
Copywriter: **Lawrence Grob**

Sales Promotion

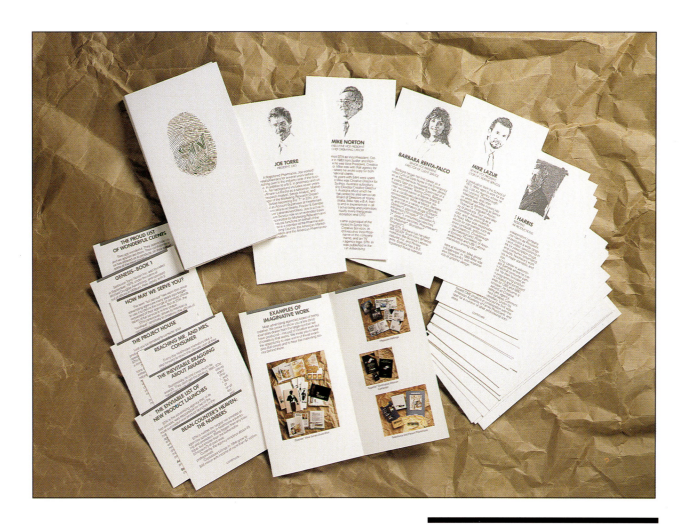

Title of Graphic: **STN Agency Brochure**
Ad Agency: **Salthouse Torre Norton, Inc.**
Client: **Salthouse Torre Norton, Inc.**
Art Director: **Mike Lazur/Neil Paulino**
Illustrator: **Paul Henry**
Photographer: **Bill Wagner/Drew Degrado**
Copywriter: **Mike Norton**

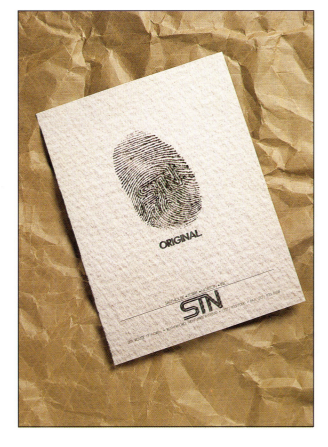

Title of Graphic: **Original — STN**
Ad Agency: **Salthouse Torre Norton, Inc.**
Client: **Salthouse Torre Norton, Inc.**
Art Director: **Mike Lazur**
Photographer: **Donato Leo**
Copywriter: **Mike Norton/Donna Lynch**

Sales Promotion

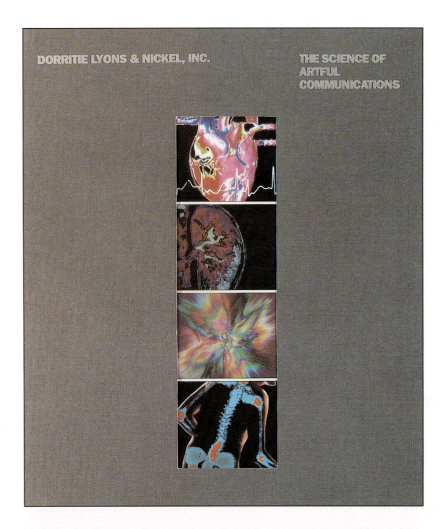

Title of Graphic: **The Science of Artful Communications**
Ad Agency: **Dorritie Lyons & Nickel**
Client: **Dorritie Lyons & Nickel**
Art Director: **Mike Lyons**
Photographer: **Various**
Copywriter: **Bill Brown/Carol Shepko**
Structural Designer: **Dorritie Lyons & Nickel**

Title of Graphic: **Abbott Corporate Profile**
Ad Agency: **Gerbig Snell/Weisheimer & Associates**
Client: **Abbott Laboratories**
Art Director: **Diane Hay**
Photographer: **Various**
Copywriter: **Traci Lance**

Sales Promotion

Title of Graphic: **NJ Association for Biomedical Research**
Ad Agency: **C & G Advertising Agency, Inc.**
Client: **NJ Association for Biomedical Research**
Art Director: **Joseph N. Caggiano**
Illustrator: **Steve Smith**
Structural Designer: **Ciba-Geigy Pharmaceuticals**

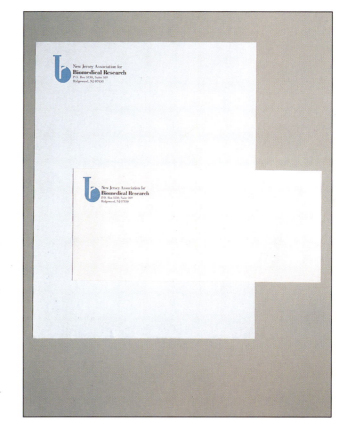

Title of Graphic: **Leadership Forum**
Ad Agency: **Pracon**
Client: **Schering Laboratories Managed Care**
Art Director: **Al Halac**
Copywriter: **Lisa Rasinski**
Structural Designer: **Carol I. Iglesias**

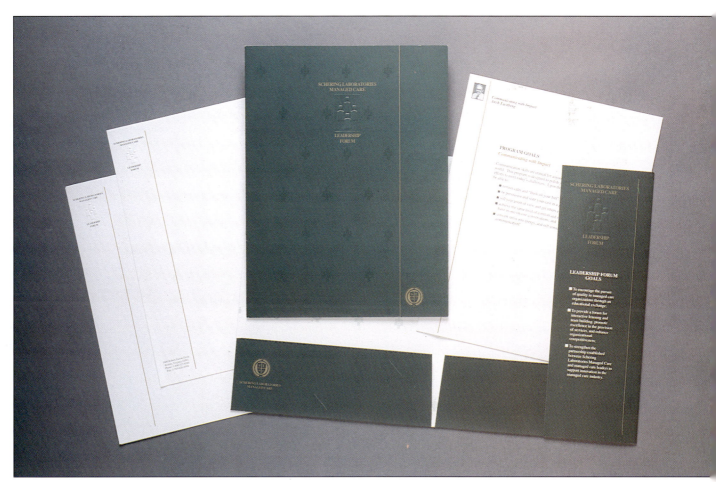

Sales Promotion

Title of Graphic: **Insight: '91 Managing the Astigmatic Patient for the Vision Tomorrow**
Ad Agency: **Pracon**
Client: **Wesley-Jessen Corp.**
Art Director: **Al Halac**
Copywriter: **Lisa Rasinski**
Structural Designer: **Carol I. Iglesias**

Title of Graphic: **Exact - Fit Factor Logo (XF)**
Ad Agency: **Leverte Associates, Inc.**
Client: **Kinamed, Inc.**
Art Director: **John Witt**
Illustrator: **Palette Studios**

Sales Promotion

Product: **M.E.D. Communications Self-Promo**
Title of Graphic: **M.E.D. Communications Journal Ad**
Ad Agency: **M.E.D. Communications**
Art Director: **Frank Kacmarsky**
Illustrator: **Steve Heimann**
Copywriter: **Susan Cathcart**

Product: **Lopressor**
Title of Graphic: **The Right Step Logo**
Ad Agency: **C & G Advertising Agency, Inc.**
Client: **Ciba-Geigy Pharmaceuticals**
Art Director: **Myrtle Johnson/Loren Mark**
Illustrator: **Tom Carnase**
Copywriter: **Kevin Purcell**

Product: **Cardiovasculars**
Title of Graphic: **Lederle Cardiovasculars**
Ad Agency: **LeDA Agency**
Client: **Lederle Laboratories**
Art Director: **Bruce Walk**
Illustrator: **Dennis Recchia**

Sales Promotion

Title of Graphic: **Ina Kramer Medical Group Eight-Postcard Mailer**
Client: **Ina Kramer's Art Director's Medical Survival Group**
Art Director: **Ina Kramer**
Copywriter: **Ina Kramer/Jami Giovanopoulos**

Title of Graphic: **Ina Kramer's Art Director's Medical Survival Kit**
Client: **Ina Kramer's Medical Artist Group**
Art Director: **Ina Kramer**
Photographer: **Various/Medical Illustrators and Photographers**
Copywriter: **Ina Kramer/ Jami Giovanopoulos**

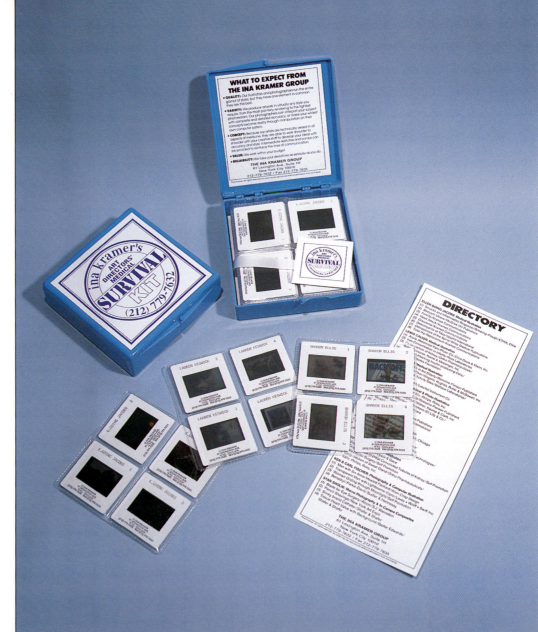

Sales Promotion

Title of Graphic: **We're Moving Mailer**
Ad Agency: **Sandler Communications**
Client: **Sandler Communications**
Art Director: **Mark Friedman**
Copywriter: **Mark Friedman**

Title of Graphic: **Corporate Identity**
Ad Agency: **Leverte Associates, Inc.**
Client: **Leverte Associates, Inc.**
Art Director: **John Witt**
Illustrator: **John Witt**

Sales Promotion

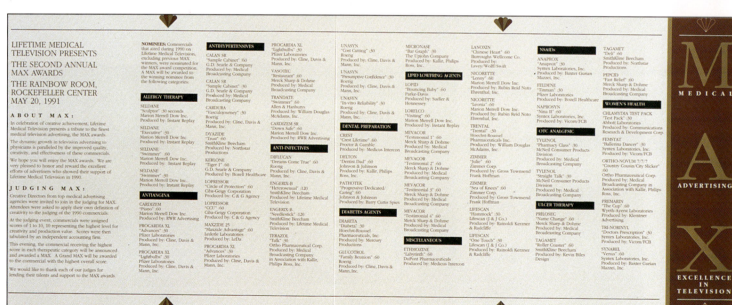

Product: **Max Awards**
Title of Graphic: **Awards Program/Stationery**
Ad Agency: **Cline, Davis & Mann, Inc.**
Client: **Lifetime Medical Television**
Art Director: **Ralph Skorge**
Copywriter: **Ed Wise**

Sales Promotion

Sales Promotion

Title of Graphic: **How Well are You Mastering the New Marketing Mix?**
Ad Agency: **Dugan/Farley Communications**
Client: **Dugan/Farley Communications**
Art Director: **Daniel W. Smith**
Illustrator: **Jon Conrad**
Copywriter: **Frank Cordasco**

Product: **Idamycin**
Title of Graphic: **There's a Universal Need in the Treatment of AML . . .**
Ad Agency: **Lally, McFarland & Pantello, Inc.**
Client: **Adria Laboratories, Inc.**
Art Director: **Audrey Sanchez**
Illustrator: **Randee Ladden**
Copywriter: **Laura Tannenbaum**

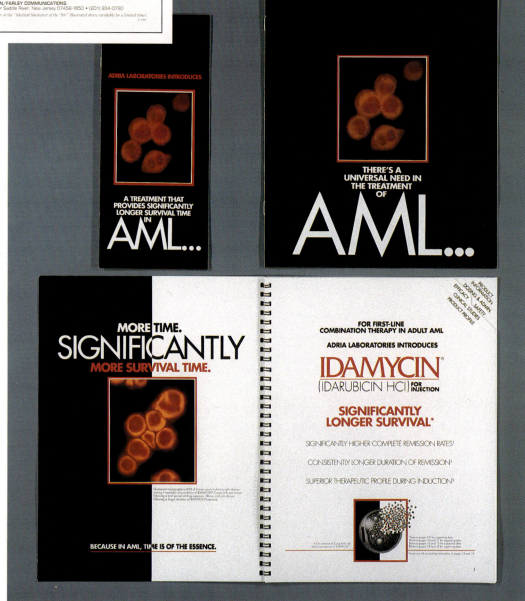

Sales Promotion

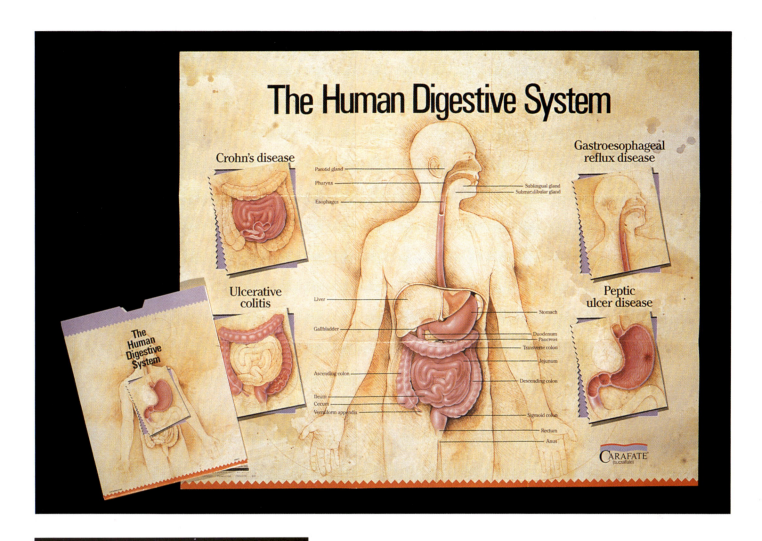

Product: **Carafate**
Title of Graphic: **Carafate Patient Education Program**
Ad Agency: **McCann Healthcare Advertising**
Client: **Marion Merrell Dow**
Art Director: **Geoff Melick**
Illustrator: **Scott Barrows**
Copywriter: **Scott Hansen**

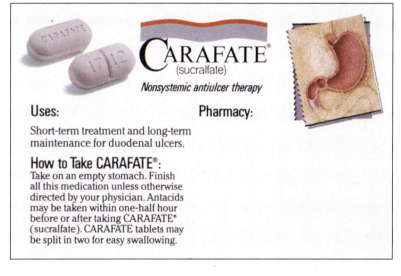

Sales Promotion

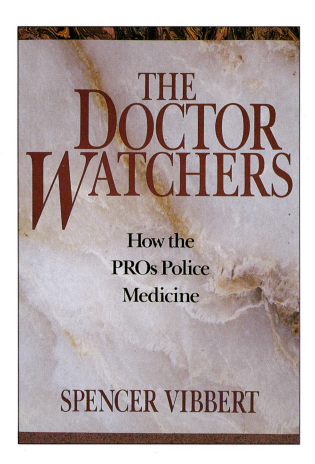

Product: **Ground Rounds**
Title of Graphic: **Ground Rounds**
Design Firm: **Lewis and Gace**
Client: **Marion Merrell Dow**
Art Director: **G. Osher/S. King**
Illustrator: **Gerd Dagne**
Photographer: **Kent Hanson**
Copywriter: **G. Dyller**

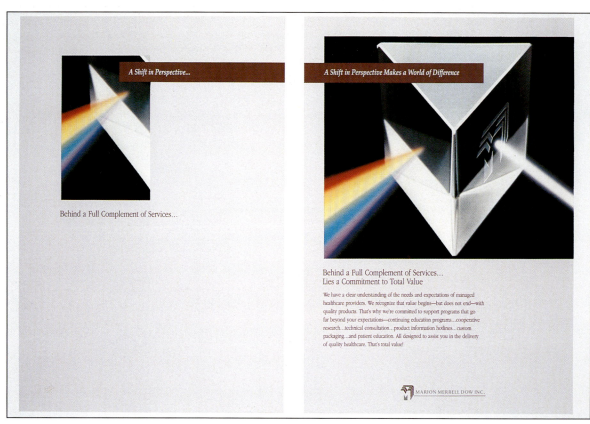

Sales Promotion

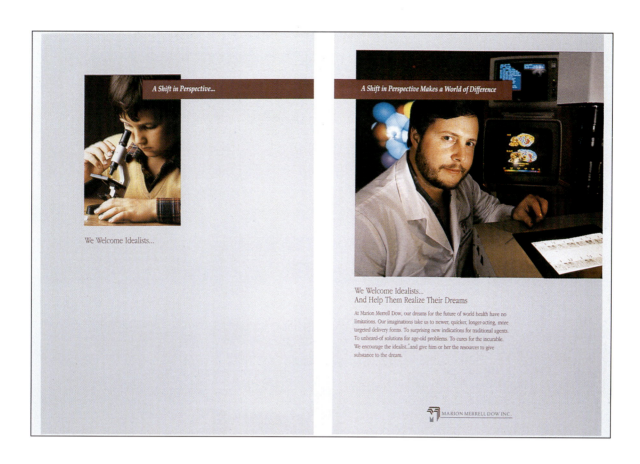

Sales Promotion

Product: **Carafate**
Title of Graphic: **Smoker Sales Aid**
Ad Agency: **McCann Healthcare Advertising**
Client: **Marion Merrell Dow**
Art Director: **Geoff Melick**
Photographer: **Bill Tucker**
Copywriter: **Scott Hansen**
Structural Designer: **Spangler Printers**

Sales Promotion

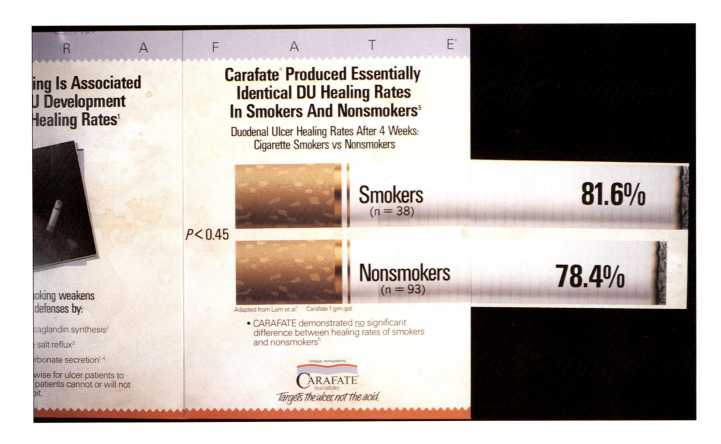

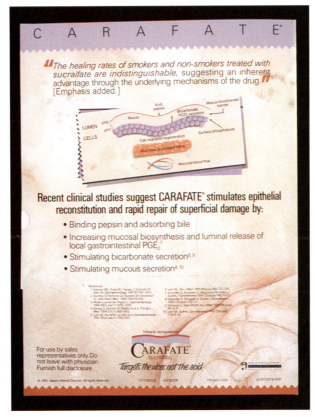

Sales Promotion

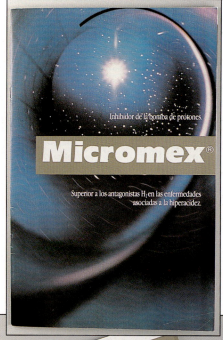
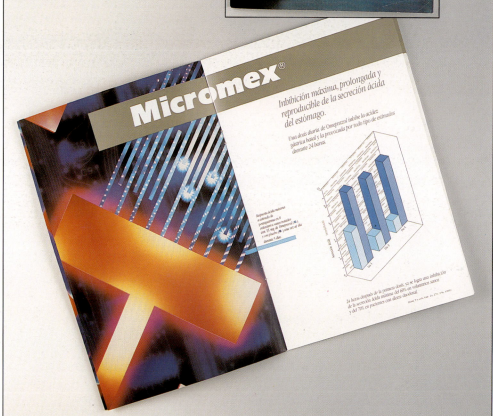

Product: **Micromex**
Title of Graphic: **Micromex**
Ad Agency: **Frederick & Valenzuela Ltda.**
Client: **Laboratorios Recalcine S.A.**
Art Director: **Cristian Frederick/Jacqueline Krause**
Photographer: **The Image Bank**

POSTERS/DISPLAYS

Pictorial, powerful, and public. Those are the words that sum up this category. Unlike the type of promotion that is designed to be seen by one individual at one point in time, posters are designed to be seen by many people at various times. Some posters are created for educational purposes. Other posters can be instructional or persuasive or may publicize specific events. Regardless of their purpose, the commonality of all posters is that they are designed to have a high impact and simplicity of message. Posters are big and bold, and this section presents those that were judged as representative of the best.

Posters/Displays

Product: **The Leksell Selector Ultrasonic Aspirator; The Leksell Gamma Knife; The Leksell Micro-Stereotactic System**
Title of Graphic: **Brainstorm; Braintrust; Brainchild; Meeting of the Minds**
Ad Agency: **Rainoldi Kerzner Radcliffe**
Client: **Elekta Instruments, Inc.**
Art Director: **Dale Kenwood**
Illustrator: **Vince Perez**
Photographer: **Dave Wilhelm**
Copywriter: **Jeremiah Treacy**

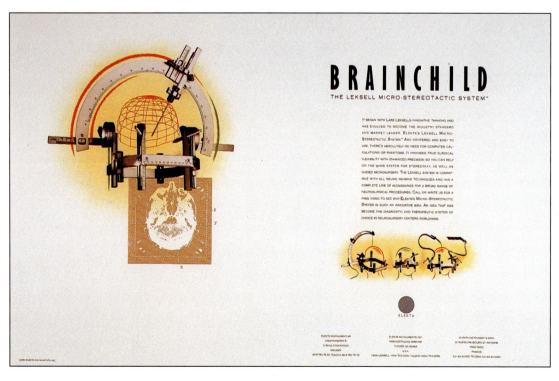

Posters/Displays

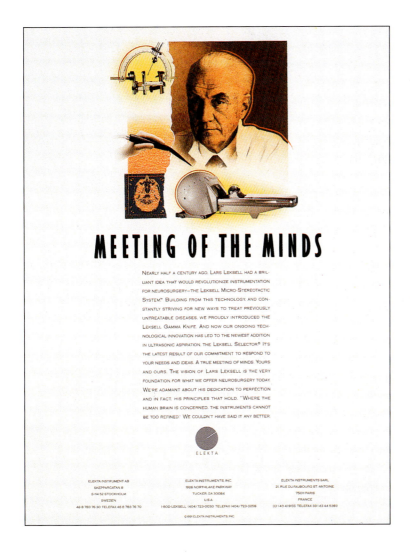

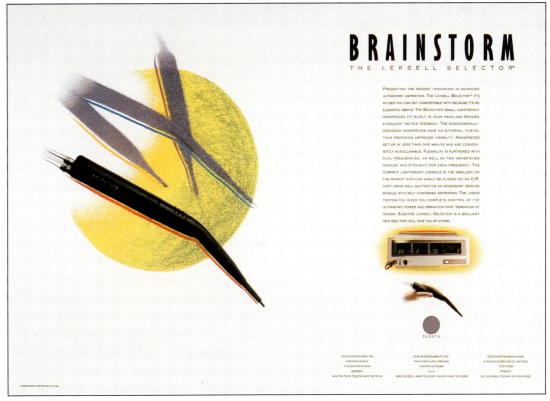

Posters/Displays

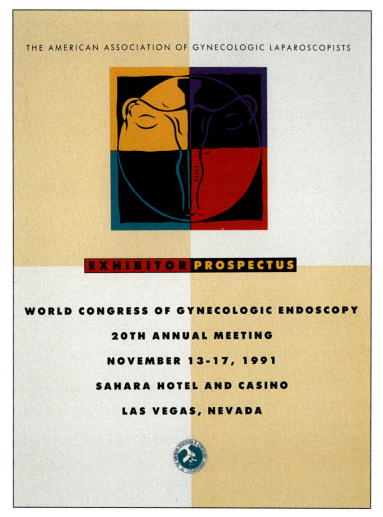

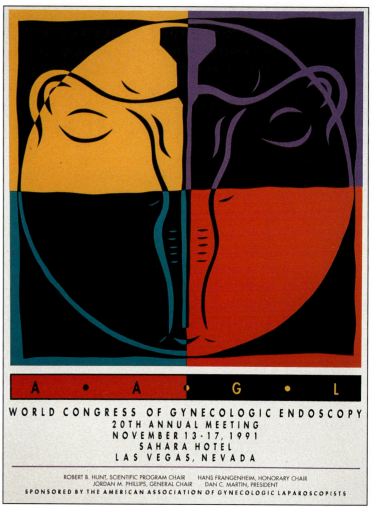

Title of Graphic: **Prospectus**
Design Firm: **Radius Graphic Design**
Client: **A.A.G.L.**
Art Director: **Steve Green**

Title of Graphic: **Poster**
Design Firm: **Radius Graphic Design**
Client: **A.A.G.L.**
Art Director: **Steve Green**

Posters/Displays

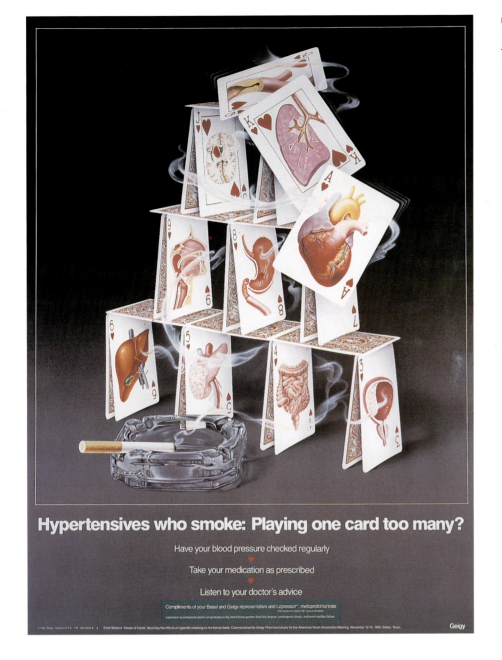

Product: **Lopresser**
Title of Graphic: **Hypertensives who Smoke**
Ad Agency: **C & G Advertising Agency, Inc.**
Client: **Ciba-Geigy Pharmaceuticals**
Art Director: **Myrtle Johnson**
Illustrator: **Enid Hatton**
Copywriter: **Kevin Purcell**

Product: **Diabeta**
Title of Graphic: **Target Organs of Diabetes**
Design Firm: **Devcom, Inc.**
Client: **Hoechst-Roussel Pharmaceuticals Inc.**
Art Director: **Amy Brent**
Illustrator: **Lewis Calver**

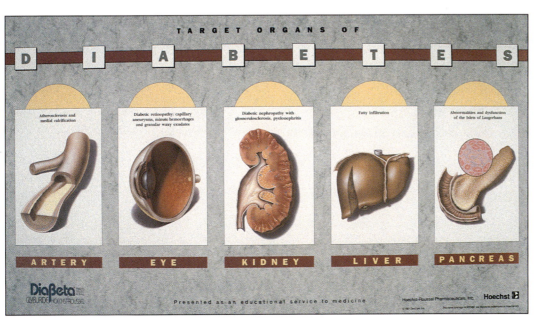

Posters/Displays

Product: **Pfizer, Inc.**
Title of Graphic: **Bringing Science to Life**
Design Firm: **Puches Design, Inc.**
Client: **Pfizer, Inc.**
Art Director: **Puches Design, Inc.**
Illustrator: **Various including Johnna Bandle, Bill Finewood**
Photographer: **Pfizer, Inc.**
Copywriter: **Pfizer, Inc.**
Structural Designer: **Puches Design, Inc.**
Exhibit Fabrication: **Display Studios, Inc.**

Posters/Displays

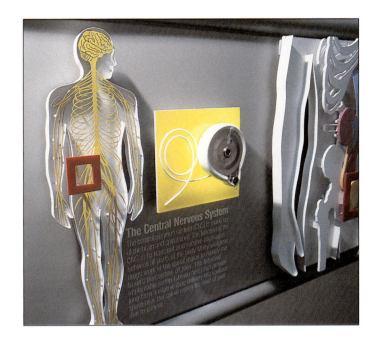

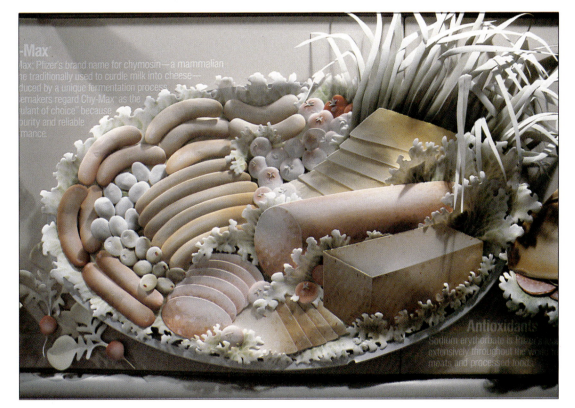

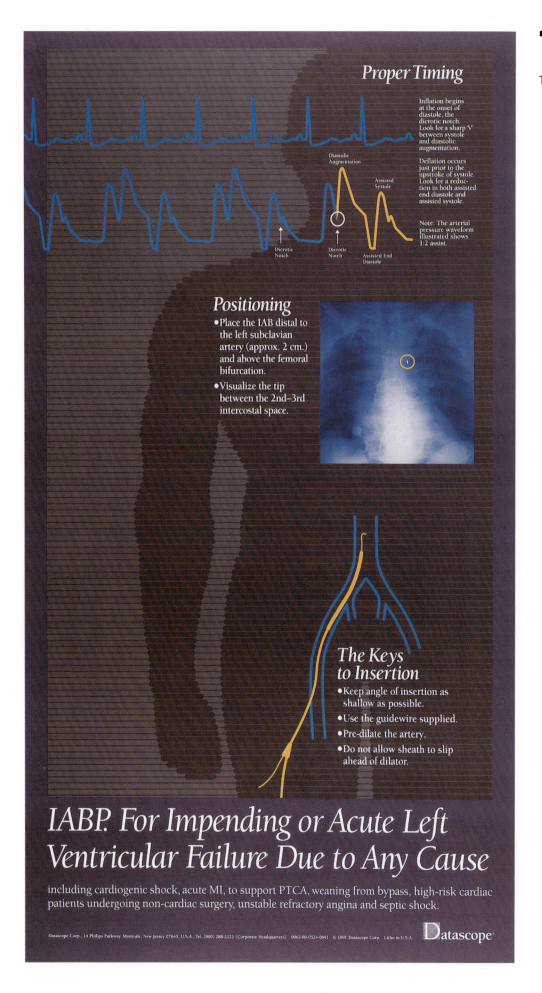

Product: **Datascope Intra Aortic Balloon Pump**
Title of Graphic: **IABP Instructional Poster**
Ad Agency: **Dick Jackson, Inc.**
Client: **Datascope Corp.**
Art Director: **Diana Wheaton/ David Lukshus**
Illustrator: **Diana Wheaton**
Copywriter: **Richard Jackson**

Product: **Minocin (minocycline HC1 pellet-filled capsules)**
Title of Graphic: **Acne Facts**
Ad Agency: **The LeDA Agency**
Client: **Lederle Laboratories**
Art Director: **Joyce Schnaufer**
Illustrator: **Dan Flanagan, Peggy Bonfiglio**
Copywriter: **Barbara Schloss**

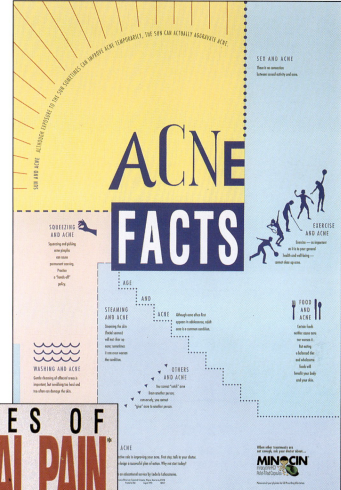

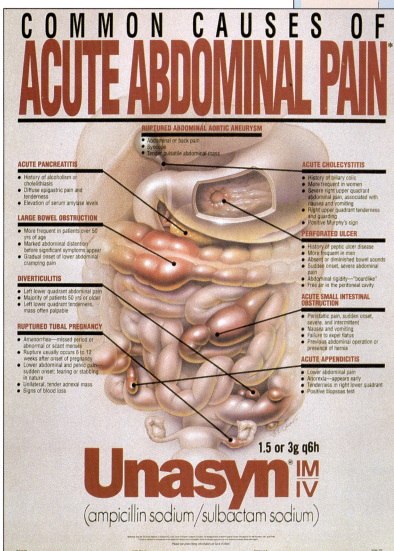

Product: **Unasyn**
Title of Graphic: **Acute Abdominal Pain**
Ad Agency: **Cline, Davis & Mann, Inc.**
Client: **Roerig**
Art Director: **Andy Moore**
Illustrator: **Lew Calver**
Copywriter: **Dave Renner**

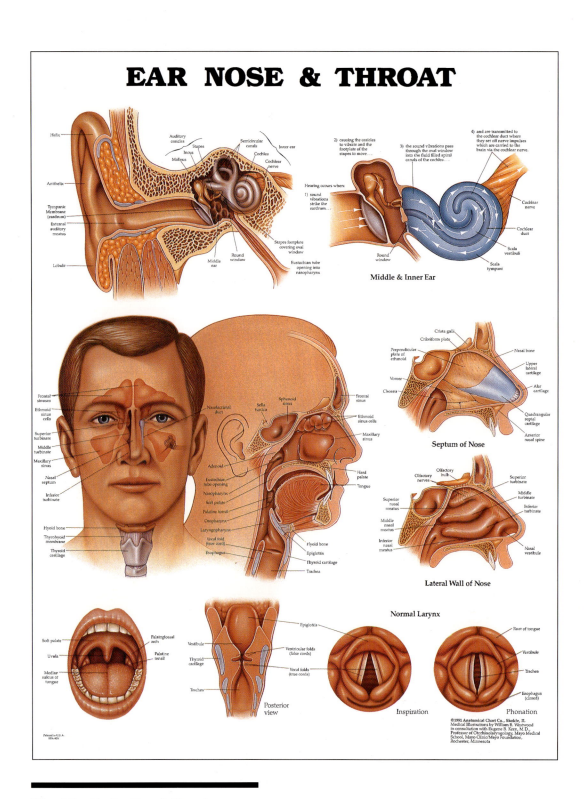

Title of Graphic: **Ear Nose & Throat**
Design Firm: **Anatomical Chart Company**
Client: **Storz Instrument Company**
Art Director: **Christine D. Young**
Illustrator: **William B. Westwood**

Posters/Displays

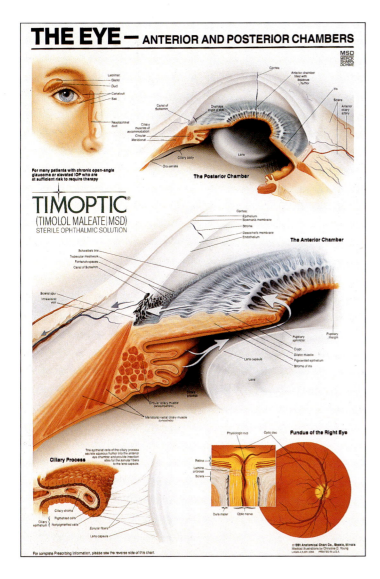

Product: **Timoptic**
Title of Graphic: **The Eye — Anterior and Posterior Chambers**
Design Firm: **Anatomical Chart Company**
Client: **Merck, Sharp & Dohme**
Art Director: **Christine D. Young**
Illustrator: **Christine D. Young**

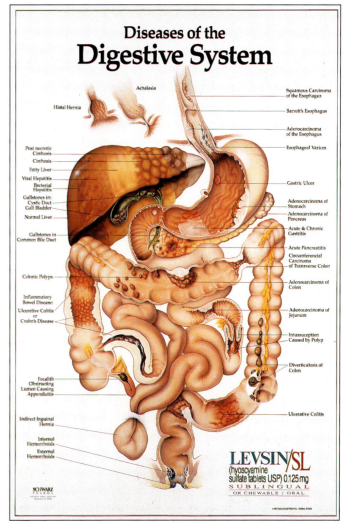

Product: **Levsin/SL**
Title of Graphic: **Diseases of the Digestive System**
Design Firm: **Anatomical Chart Company**
Client: **Schwarz Pharma**
Art Director: **Christine D. Young**
Illustrator: **Michael W. Carroll**

Posters/Displays

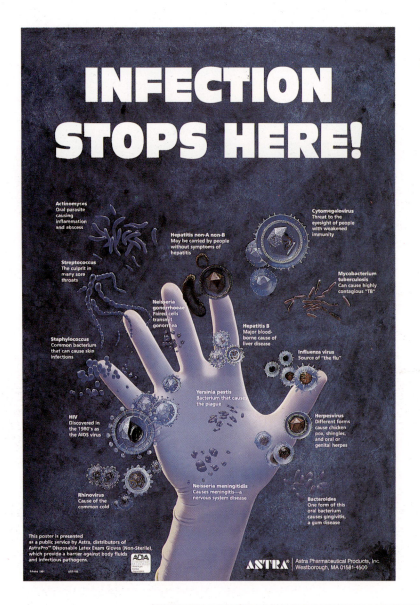

Product: **AstraPro Gloves**
Title of Graphic: **Infection Stops Here!**
Ad Agency: **Leverte Associates, Inc.**
Client: **Astra Pharmaceutical Products, Inc.**
Art Director: **Reiner/Witt**
Illustrator: **George Schwenk**
Copywriter: **Mascolini/Witt**

Product: **Nasalide**
Title of Graphic: **Periodic Table of Allergens**
Ad Agency: **Vicom/FCB**
Client: **Syntex**
Art Director: **Jeffrey Hicken**
Illustrator: **Derek Grinnell**
Copywriter: **Bob Finkel/Janet Conley**

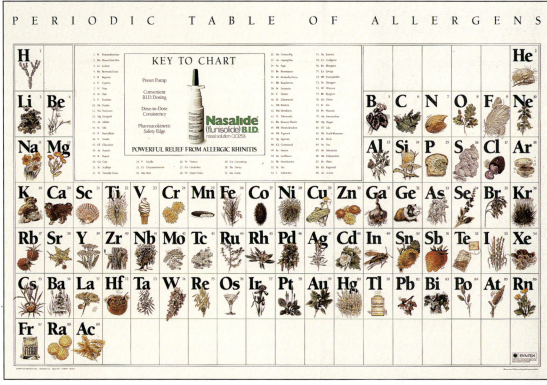

EDITORIAL

This is the realm of the artist, where the graphic can communicate either a single thought or an entire story. Here are the pictures that can reprise or replace the written word. Independently they can evoke a specific image, an emotion, or a memory. Through the images envisioned by art directors and the techniques employed by different artists, illustrators and photographers, we can view the DNA of a single cell, learn the correct placement of a catheter, experience a migraine headache, or view the miracle of conception.

Editorial

Product: **The Good Health Magazine**
Title of Graphic: **Sidelined by Loneliness**
Client: **The New York Times**
Art Director: **Nancy V. Kent**
Photographer: **Bill Binzen**
Copywriter: **Richard Flaste**

Title of Graphic: **Screening the Tests that Detect Cancer**
Art Director: **Nancy V. Kent**
Photographer: **Burk Uzzle**
Copywriter: **Elisabeth Rosenthal**

Title of Graphic: **Dramatic Progress Against Depression**
Art Director: **Nancy V. Kent**
Photographer: **Frank Viva**
Copywriter: **Miriam Shuchman and Michael S. Wilkes**

Title of Graphic: **Is There a Time Bomb Ticking in Women's Breasts?**
Client: **Longevity**
Art Director: **Carveth Kramer**
Photographer: **Tom Arma**
Editor: **Rona Cherry**

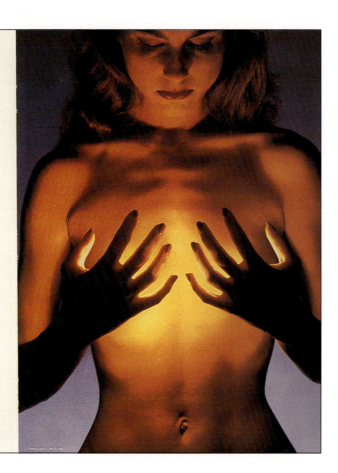

Editorial

193

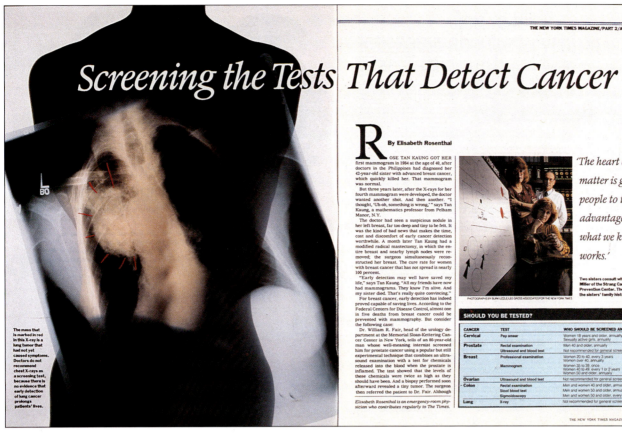

THE NEW YORK TIMES MAGAZINE/PART 2/APRIL 28, 1991

Screening the Tests That Detect Cancer

By Elisabeth Rosenthal

ROSE TAN KAUNG GOT HER first mammogram in 1984 at the age of 40, after doctors in the Philippines had diagnosed her 42-year-old sister with advanced breast cancer, which quickly killed her. That mammogram was normal.

But three years later, after the X-rays for her fourth mammogram were developed, the doctor wanted another shot. And then another. "I thought, 'Uh-oh, something is wrong,'" says Tan Kaung, a mathematics professor from Pelham Manor, N.Y.

The doctor had seen a suspicious nodule in her left breast, far too deep and tiny to be felt. It was the kind of bad news that makes the time, cost and discomfort of early cancer detection worthwhile. A month later Tan Kaung had a modified radical mastectomy, in which the entire breast and nearby lymph nodes were removed; the surgeon simultaneously reconstructed her breast. The cure rate for women with breast cancer that has not spread is nearly 100 percent.

"Early detection may well have saved my life," says Tan Kaung. "All my friends have now had mammograms. They know I'm alive. And my sister died. That's really quite convincing."

For breast cancer, early detection has indeed proved capable of saving lives. According to the Federal Centers for Disease Control, almost one in five deaths from breast cancer could be prevented with mammography. But consider the following case:

Dr. William R. Fair, head of the urology department at the Memorial Sloan-Kettering Cancer Center in New York, tells of an 80-year-old man whose well-meaning internist screened him for prostate cancer using a popular but still experimental technique that combines an ultrasound examination with a test for chemicals released into the blood when the prostate is inflamed. The test showed that the levels of these chemicals were twice as high as they should have been. And a biopsy performed soon afterward revealed a tiny tumor. The surgeon then referred the patient to Dr. Fair. Although

Elisabeth Rosenthal is an emergency-room physician who contributes regularly to The Times.

'The heart of the matter is getting people to take advantage of what we know works.'

Two sisters consult with Dr. Daniel Miller of the Strang Cancer Prevention Center. The chart shows the sisters' family history of cancer.

SHOULD YOU BE TESTED?

CANCER	TEST	WHO SHOULD BE SCREENED AND HOW OFTEN
Cervical	Pap smear	Women 18 years and older, annually Sexually active girls, annually
Prostate	Rectal examination	Men 40 and older, annually
	Ultrasound and blood test	Not recommended for general screening
Breast	Professional examination	Women 20 to 40, every 3 years Women over 40, annually
	Mammogram	Women 35 to 39, once Women 40 to 49, every 1 or 2 years Women 50 and older, annually
Ovarian	Ultrasound and blood test	Not recommended for general screening
Colon	Rectal examination	Men and women 40 and older, annually
	Stool blood test	Men and women 50 and older, annually
	Sigmoidoscopy	Men and women 50 and older, every 3 to 5 years
Lung	X-ray	Not recommended for general screening

THE NEW YORK TIMES MAGAZINE/PART 2/OCTOBER 7, 1990

Dramatic Progress Against Depression

The success of new drugs is prompting debate on their overuse—and the value of talk therapy.

By Miriam Shuchman and Michael S. Wilkes

BY ALL ACCOUNTS DR. Raphael J. Osheroff, a kidney specialist, had a successful medical practice in a suburb of Washington. But then he became seriously depressed. The sadness grew worse and worse and made it increasingly difficult for him to work. This was 13 years ago. After two years of therapy, the 41-year-old doctor admitted himself to Chestnut Lodge, a private psychiatric hospital in the area, where he was treated daily with intensive psychotherapy. His doctors did not offer him antidepressant medication, even though he says he and his family repeatedly requested it.

After seven months, Dr. Osheroff left Chestnut Lodge and went to Silver Hill, a private psychiatric hospital in New Canaan, Conn., where he received medication and fully recovered within a few months. But he says he paid a huge price for the delay in receiving the antidepressant drugs: "I was waking up at 4 every morning, pacing so much that my feet deteriorated. I lost 40 pounds, I deteriorated mentally and physically, I lost a whole life. I had a million-dollar medical practice, I lost that. I lost my status in the medical community, I lost the respect of my patients, I even lost contact with my children."

Dr. Osheroff sued the Chestnut Lodge doctors for malpractice, arguing that proper care should have included medication. Two years ago he won an out-of-court settlement, which many psychiatrists now view as a landmark in the treatment of clinical depression. A year after the settlement, the National Institutes of Mental Health completed a major research project showing medications to be more effective than psychotherapy for the most severe forms of clinical depression. Together, the N.I.M.H. study and Dr. Osheroff's case have sparked a vigorous debate over how people with this illness should be treated.

Clinical depression is a sadness that is overwhelming and long lasting, and is often accompanied by thoughts of suicide as well as sleeplessness, loss of appetite and an inability to function. About one in every five adults in the United States experiences a clinical depression at some point during his or her life. Many are misdiagnosed by doctors or therapists who fail to recognize the symptoms. Others blame themselves for their condition and do not even seek professional advice.

But experts say the problem can be effectively treated — and not only in those whose depression makes them unable to function. Today, medications as well as therapy are also being offered to people with chronic depression, a milder form of the disorder that can persist for years in people who are able to work, sleep and eat, but cannot remember when they last felt happy.

By 1970, hundreds of studies showed that antidepressant drugs work for about 80 percent of patients, and can cut the duration of the illness down to a few months. These drugs have

(Continued on Page 30)

Miriam Shuchman, M.D., is a psychiatrist at the University of California at San Francisco. Michael S. Wilkes, M.D., is a physician at the University of California at Los Angeles.

Common Categories Of Depression

- **MAJOR DEPRESSION:** Intense and long-lasting feelings of sadness and despair that can lead, in severe cases, to suicide; can cause loss of appetite and inability to sleep, concentrate or function normally.

- **MANIC-DEPRESSIVE ILLNESS:** Recurrent episodes of major depression and mania; the manic phase is characterized by loquacity, enormous energy and unrealistic, often delusional notions about oneself and one's ability.

- **ATYPICAL DEPRESSION:** Similar to major depression, but some key symptoms are different — for instance, instead of sleeping less, atypical depressives sleep more than usual.

- **CHRONIC DEPRESSION:** A milder form of major depression that persists for years; people with this disorder constantly feel unhappy with themselves and their lives, though they are able to function.

- **SEASONAL DEPRESSION:** Appears in late fall or early winter, with all the symptoms of a major depression, and disappears in the spring or early summer.

Editorial

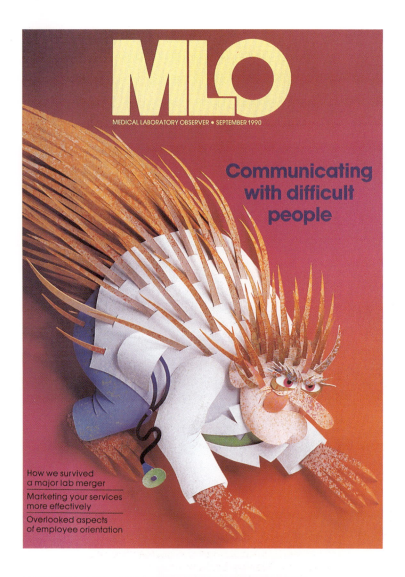

Title of Graphic: **Communicating with Difficult People**
Design Firm: **Medical Economics Publishing**
Client: **Medical Laboratory Observer**
Art Director: **Kathy Cuddihy**
Illustrator: **Leo Monahan**
Photographer: **Stephen E. Munz**

Title of Graphic: **Laboratory Salaries**
Client: **Medical Laboratory Observer**
Art Director: **Christie Wilson**
Illustrator: **Christie Wilson**
Photographer: **Stephen E. Munz**
Sculpture: **Joan Steiner**

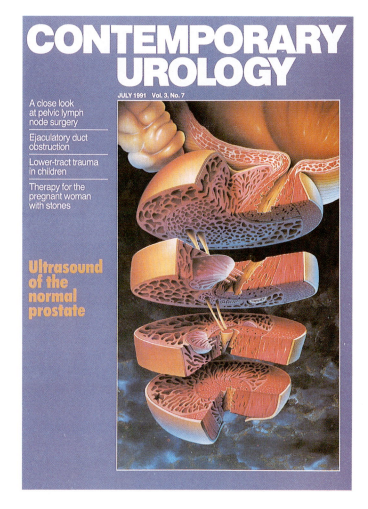

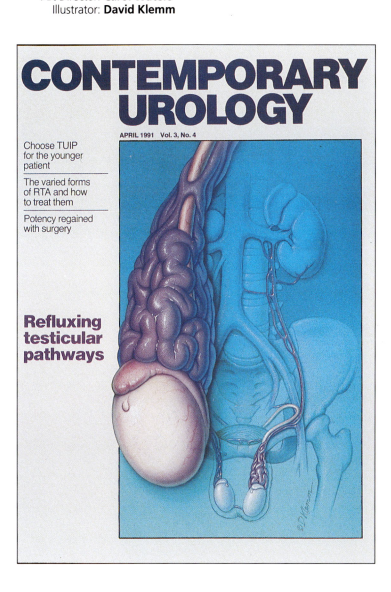

Title of Graphic: **Refluxing Testicular Pathways**
Design Firm: **Medical Economics Publishing**
Client: **Contemporary Urology**
Art Director: **Carol Waters**
Illustrator: **David Klemm**

Title of Graphic: **Ultrasound of the Normal Prostate**
Design Firm: **Medical Economics**
Client: **Contemporary Urology**
Art Director: **Carol Waters**
Illustrator: **Keith Kasnot**

Editorial

Title of Graphic: **Anaphylaxis**
Client: **Patient Care Magazine**
Art Director: **Nancy L. Stetler**
Illustrator: **Kevin Somerville**

Title of Graphic: **Communicating the Bad News**
Design Firm: **Medical Economics Publishing**
Client: **Business & Health**
Art Director: **Carol Waters**
Illustrator: **Brian Ajhar**

Editorial

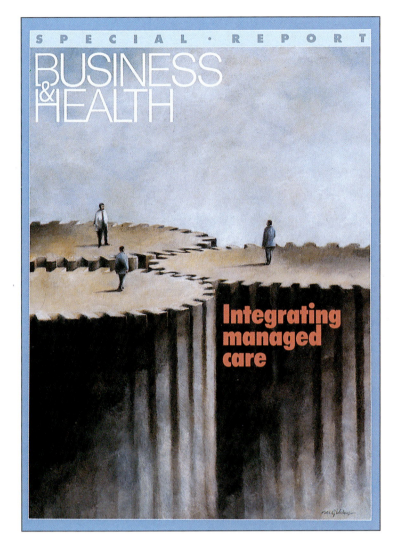

Title of Graphic: **Integrating Managed Care**
Design Firm: **Medical Economics Publishing**
Client: **Business & Health Special Report**
Art Director: **Carol Waters**
Illustrator: **Michael Gibbs**

Product: **Medical Economics Cover**
Title of Graphic: **Can More Doctors be Lured into Medicaid?**
Design Firm: **Medical Economics Publishing**
Client: **Medical Economics**
Art Director: **Roger Dowd**
Illustrator: **Joan Steiner**
Photographer: **Walter Wick**
Copywriter: **Carol Stevens**

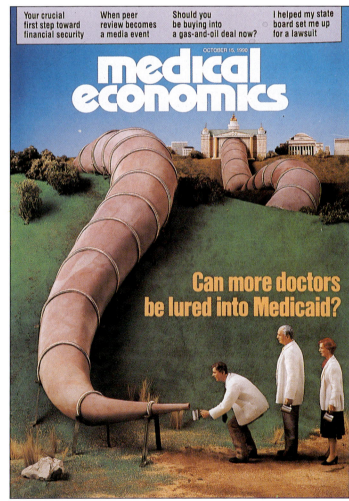

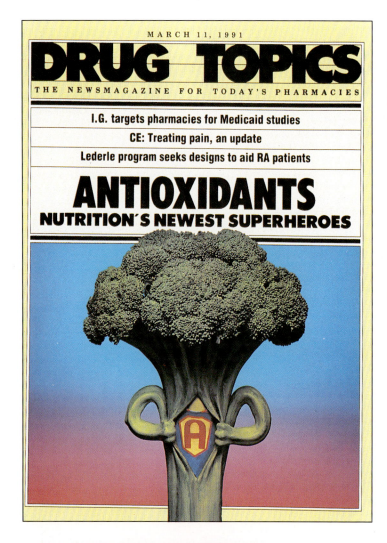

Title of Graphic: **Antioxidants: Nutrition's Newest Superheroes**
Design Firm: **Medical Economics Publishing**
Client: **Drug Topics Magazine**
Art Director: **Thomas Darnsteadt**
Photographer: **Stephen E. Munz**
Copywriter: **Val Cardinale**
Structural Designer: **Joan Steiner**

Title of Graphic: **Theft: How Safe are Pharmacies?**
Design Firm: **Medical Economics Publishing**
Client: **Drug Topics Magazine**
Art Director: **Thomas Darnsteadt**
Illustrator: **Howard Fine**
Copywriter: **Val Cardinale**

Editorial

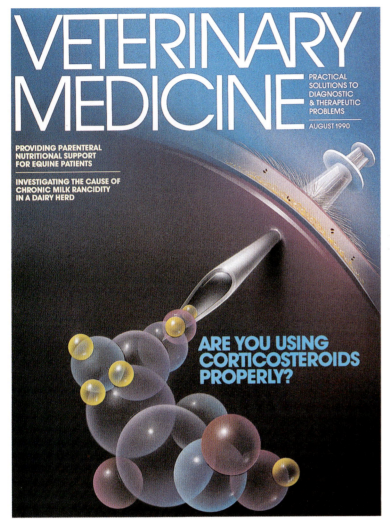

Product: **Veterinary Medicine**
Title of Graphic: **Are You Using Corticosteroids Properly?**
Design Firm: **Veterinary Medicine Publishing Co.**
Client: **Veterinary Medicine**
Art Director: **Mark Eisler**
Illustrator: **Edmond Alexander**
Copywriter: **Jennifer Gaumnitz**

Product: **Veterinary Medicine**
Title of Graphic: **Handling the Victims of Spinal Cord Trauma**
Design Firm: **Veterinary Medicine Publishing Co.**
Client: **Veterinary Medicine**
Art Director: **Mark Eisler**
Illustrator: **Edmond Alexander**
Copywriter: **Jennifer Gaumnitz**

Editorial

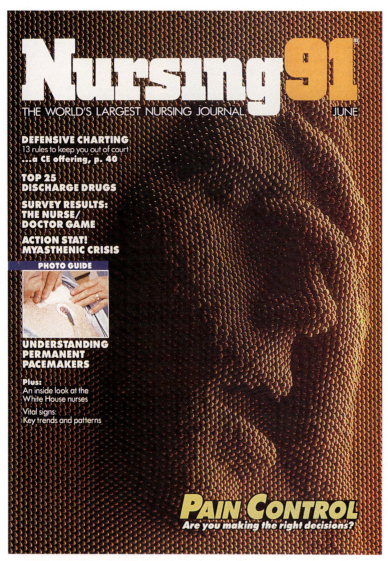

Product: **Nursing 91 Cover**
Title of Graphic: **Pain Control**
Art Director: **Ed Rosanio**
Photographer: **Impact Studios**

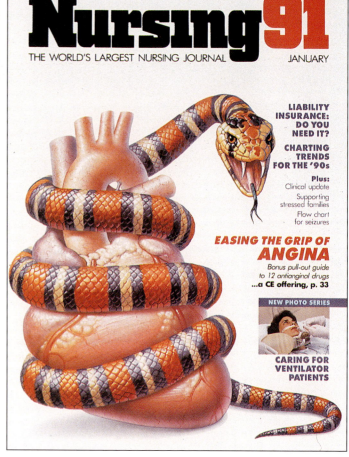

Product: **Nursing 91 Cover**
Title of Graphic: **Loosening the Grip of Anginal Pain**
Art Director: **Ed Rosanio**
Illustrator: **Walter Sturat**

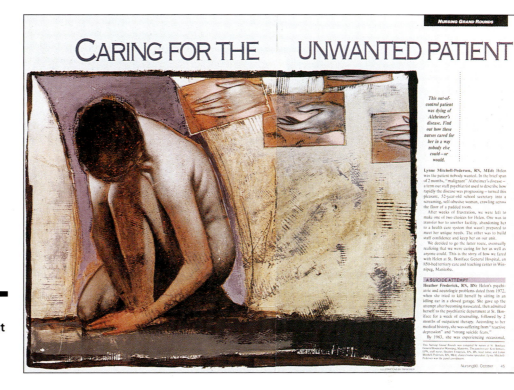

Title of Graphic: **Caring for the Unwanted Patient**
Client: **Nursing 90**
Art Director: **Ed Rosanio**
Illustrator: **Tim Bower**

Title of Graphic: **Caring for the Suicidal Patient**
Client: **Nursing 91**
Art Director: **Nancy McDonald**
Illustrator: **Tim Bower**

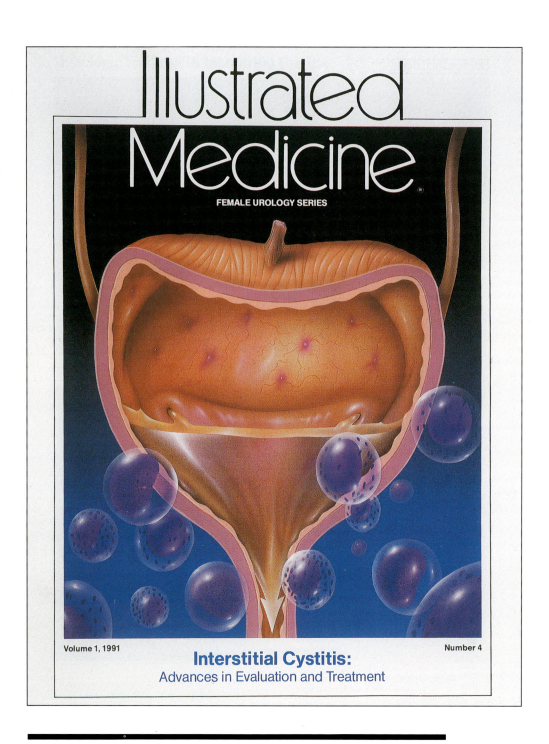

Product: **Illustrated Medicine, Female Urology Series**
Title of Graphic: **Interstitial Cystitis: Advances in Evaluation and Treatment**
Design Firm: **Alexander & Turner**
Client: **ICI Pharma/Stuart Pharmaceuticals**
Art Director: **Edmond Alexander & Cynthia Turner**
Illustrator: **Edmond Alexander & Cynthia Turner**
Copywriter: **Nancy Agresta Weissflog**
Structural Designer: **Design/Type Inc./Larry Klein**

CLINICAL DIALOGUE
IN FEMALE UROLOGY

Interstitial Cystitis:
Advances in Evaluation and Treatment

Mickey Karram, MD, and C. Lowell Parsons, MD

In this issue of *Illustrated Medicine* a gynecologist and a urologist discuss a very large group of female patients with lower urinary tract symptomatology that is frequently as frustrating to the physician as to the patient. Hopefully, a current rise in interest in the disease will improve the outlook for treatment and perhaps cure of this entity, although no magic potion is available at present.

Illustrated Medicine: What is the clinical distinction between patients with urethral syndrome and those with interstitial cystitis or painful bladder syndrome as interstitial cystitis is sometimes referred to?

Dr Parsons: That's a tough question. I probably could have given a better answer 10 years ago when urethral syndrome was a more popular diagnosis and interstitial cystitis was considered extremely rare.

Dr Karram is Assistant Professor of Obstetrics and Gynecology, University of Cincinnati School of Medicine, Cincinnati, Ohio. He is also Director of Gynecologic Urology, Good Samaritan Hospital, Cincinnati, Ohio.

Today the main distinction between the two entities is severity. Most persons with urethral syndrome probably have a mild form of interstitial cystitis.[1] These persons will have low-grade, intermittent symptoms of urgency, frequency, suprapubic pain, and sterile urine. In addition, they have a tendency toward spontaneous remission. Like interstitial cystitis, urethral syndrome seems to be precipitated and aggravated by true bladder infection. But interstitial cystitis is a more persistently symptomatic disease, with more urgency, more frequency, more pain, and is usually not characterized by significant or prolonged remission.

Dr Karram: I agree with Dr Parsons. This *is* a difficult question, especially since urethral syndrome is not a well-appreciated entity in many quarters. We use the term "urethral syndrome" to describe patients who have lower urinary tract symptoms of urgency, frequency, dysuria, and suprapubic discomfort, in the absence of any objective findings of urethral or bladder abnormality. It's kind of a "wastebasket" diagnosis.

The idea that urethral syndrome is an early form of interstitial cystitis is very intriguing. Some researchers in the United Kingdom[2] have recently reported objective evidence showing that these patients may be infected with aerobic or noncoliform organisms which we are not commonly culturing for.

Several years ago, Stamm showed that urethral syndrome was associated with either a low bacterial count in voided urine or a chlamydial infection.[3] Since that time there has been a lot of press about chlamydial infection causing the "urethral syndrome," but we have not been very successful in identifying these organisms in our patients. Certain patients, however, do seem to subjectively respond to empiric tetracycline, and this would lead some credence to the idea that noncoliform organisms, possibly sexually transmitted, are causing this lower urinary tract dysfunction.

Epidemiology

IM: How prevalent is interstitial cystitis and in what age groups does it usually occur?

Dr Parsons: Our data base is now approaching 400 patients, so we have a lot of input. Oravisto in Helsinki, Finland, in the 1960s and 1970s, traced the prevalence of moderate to

continued

Dr Parsons is Professor of Surgery-Urology, UCSD Medical Center, University of California, San Diego.

Histologic Findings in Interstitial Cystitis

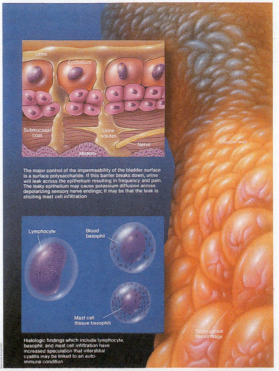

The major control of the impermeability of the bladder surface is a surface polysaccharide. If this barrier breaks down, urine will leak across the epithelium resulting in frequency and pain. The leaky epithelium may cause potassium diffusion across depolarizing sensory nerve endings; it may be that the leak is eliciting mast cell infiltration

Histologic findings which include lymphocyte, basophil, and mast cell infiltration have increased speculation that interstitial cystitis may be linked to an auto-immune condition

Diagnosis of Interstitial Cystitis

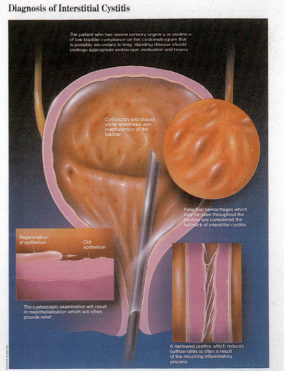

The patient who has severe sensory urgency or evidence of low bladder compliance on her cystometrogram that is possibly secondary to long-standing disease should undergo appropriate endoscopic evaluation and biopsy

Cystoscopy and biopsy under anesthesia with overdistention of the bladder

Petechial hemorrhages which may be seen throughout the bladder are considered the hallmark of interstitial cystitis

Regeneration of epithelium

Old epithelium

The cystoscopic examination will result in reepithelialization which will often provide relief

A narrowed urethra which reduces outflow rates is often a result of the recurring inflammatory process

Editorial

Product: **Managed Medicine**
Title of Graphic: **Balancing Patient Satisfaction and High-Quality Care**
Design Firm: **Kasnot Medical Illustration**
Client: **ICI Pharmaceuticals Group**
Art Director: **Keith Kasnot**
Illustrator: **Keith Kasnot**
Copywriter: **Nancy Agresta Weissflog**
Structural Designer: **Design/Type Inc.**

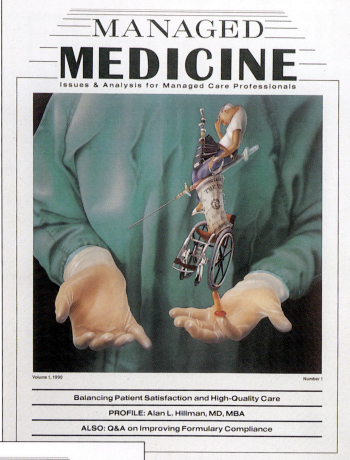

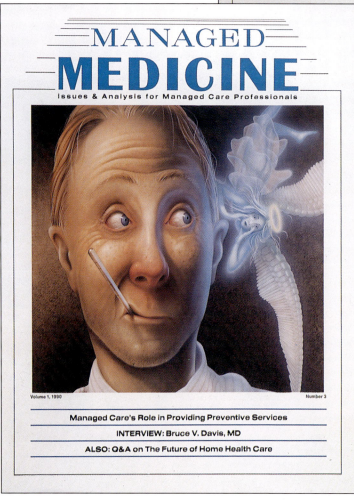

Product: **Managed Medicine**
Title of Graphic: **Managed Care's Role in Providing Preventive Services**
Design Firm: **Kasnot Medical Illustration**
Client: **ICI Pharmaceuticals Group**
Art Director: **Keith Kasnot**
Illustrator: **Keith Kasnot**
Copywriter: **Nancy Agresta Weissflog**
Structural Designer: **Design/Type Inc.**

Editorial

205

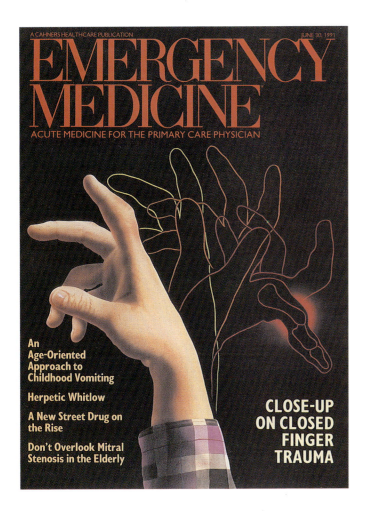

Title of Graphic: **Closed Finger Trauma**
Client: **Emergency Medicine Magazine**
Art Director: **Lois Erlacher**
Illustrator: **E.T. Steadman**

Title of Graphic: **Undoing a Summer's Worth of Sun Damage**
Client: **Longevity**
Art Director: **Carveth Kramer**
Photographer: **Henry Wolf**
Editor: **Rona Cherry**

Editorial

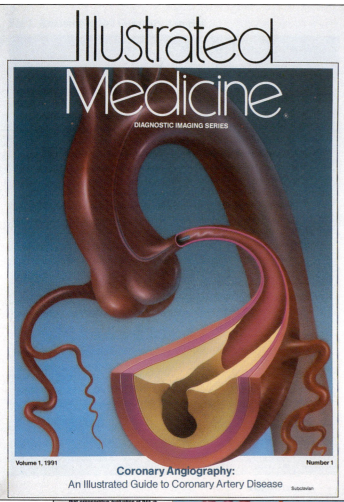

Product: **Illustrated Medicine, Diagnostic Imaging Series**
Title of Graphic: **Coronary Angiography: An Illustrated Guide to Coronary Artery Disease**
Design Firm: **Alexander & Turner**
Client: **Nycomed Imaging**
Art Director: **Edmond Alexander/Cynthia Turner**
Illustrator: **Edmond Alexander/Cynthia Turner**
Copywriter: **Nancy Agresta Weissflog**
Structural Designer: **Design/Type Inc./Larry Klein**

that preoperative evaluation of IMA integrity be part of the diagnostic coronary angiographic procedure especially if previous chest surgery or trauma has occurred. In the evaluation of the IMA graft, it is important to remember that more proximal subclavian lesions may limit flow even if the graft itself is normal (Fig 12).

Dynamic Coronary Obstruction

• **Spasm.** Coronary vasospasm may occur in vessels without obvious underlying disease. In such cases a clinical syndrome including the occurrence of profound symptoms compatible with ischemia will present a diagnostic challenge.[18] While the absence of angiographic evidence of significant coronary obstruction in a patient with ST elevation during a symptomatic episode is prima facie evidence of spasm, electrocardiographic confirmation may be unavailable. When such is the case provocative testing with ergonovine may be indicated. Graduated amounts of this drug are given intravenously under angiographic and electrocardiographic monitoring. Because intense spasm and ischemia may result, it is essential that the drug be given carefully, that parenteral nitroglycerin be available (preferably to be given intracoronary), and that facilities for emergency pacemaking and resuscitation are on hand. The occurrence of localized coronary constriction and the appearance of typical ECG changes indicate a positive ergonovine test (Fig 13). Diffuse vasoconstriction of the coronary arteries is a nonspecific response to the drug.

Recently, attention has been directed at the provocation of spasm by a variety of influences (exercise, adenosine, serotonin) at the site of the atherosclerotic lesions.[19] It has been suggested that such abnormal reactivity may provide an explanation for the occurrence of ischemia in the absence of a "significant" lesion on routine angiography.

• **Myocardial bridging.** Segments of the epicardial coronary artery may course under myocardium and be constricted during contraction of the heart. In such situations, the angiogram reveals systolic compression of that segment of the vessel (usually the LAD) (Fig 14). Since myocardial blood flow is considered to occur during diastole, the clinical effects of bridging have for the most part been considered inconsequential. However, there have been situations in which ischemia has been documented during exertion usually in association with high heart rates.[20] In some cases surgical "lysing" of the overlying myocardial band has been performed. Bridging of septal perforating arteries may be seen in a variety of situations in which left ventricular hypertrophy occurs—especially hypertrophic cardiomyopathy. Myocardial bridging should be differentiated from kinks or bends in the artery that are not flow restrictive.

Other Acquired Coronary Disorders

• **Thrombosis and embolization.** Over the last decade the critical role played by coronary thrombosis in the pathophysiology of acute myocardial infarction has been elucidated. As suggested above, thrombus formation also appears to underlie unstable angina pectoris. Thrombosis usually occurs at a site of coronary narrowing, although it may occur in angiographically normal vessels (Fig 15). It is likely that rupture of the atherosclerotic plaque incites a series of events which includes platelet aggregation, vasospasm, and thrombosis. In many cases it is difficult to angiographically distinguish layered clot from an atherosclerotic lesion. The body's own thrombolytic system may lyse thrombi as may the administration of a variety of therapeutic agents.[21] The interaction between vasospasm and thrombosis is currently being intensively studied.

Embolism to the coronary artery may occur from prosthetic heart valves, left atrial or left ventricular thrombi, or be iatrogenic from the angiographic catheter itself. Such an event may present as acute myocardial infarction and be difficult to definitively diagnose even with typical angiographic findings of abrupt vessel occlusion or filling defect. A source, association with other systemic emboli, and a compatible clinical scenario (for example, abrupt cessation of atrial fibrillation, inadequate anticoagulation of a prosthetic valve, etc) support the diagnosis of embolism. Not infrequently, distal embolization of coronary thrombus to a collateralized territory accompanies thrombolytic therapy or catheter intervention. This may result in ischemia and infarction.

• **Aneurysms.** Dilatation of a coronary artery may present in a number of morphologic patterns (Fig 16). The atherosclerotic process may produce enlargement of a vessel and obstruction. Diffuse fusiform dilatations (coronary ectasia)—which themselves are probably inconsequential—may be seen in patients with symptoms produced by concomitant discrete narrowings (Fig 17).[22] Rarely saccular aneurysms, sometimes quite large, may occur (Fig 18). In such cases the possibility of rupture must be considered. Angioplasty may result in small eccentric aneurysm formation.

Coronary aneurysms may also be due to trauma, infections, metabolic, or

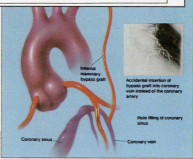
Fig 11. Angiogram showing graft placed inappropriately into a coronary vein.

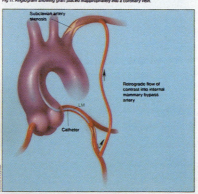
Fig 12. Internal mammary artery (IMA) graft to stenotic subclavian artery.

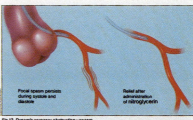
Fig 13. Dynamic coronary obstruction—spasm.

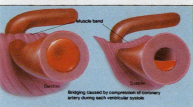
Fig 14. Dynamic coronary obstruction—myocardial bridging.

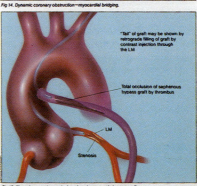
Fig 15. Thrombus causing occlusion of saphenous vein bypass graft.

Editorial

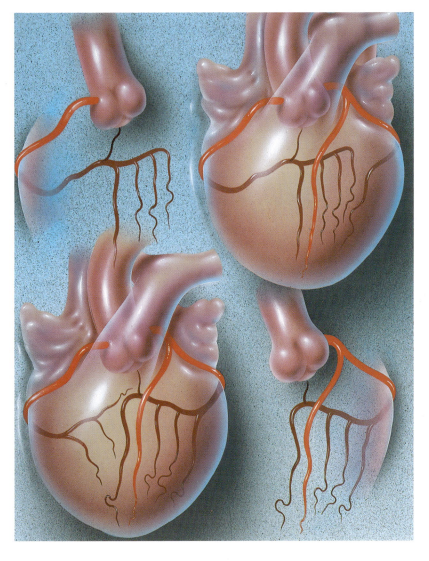
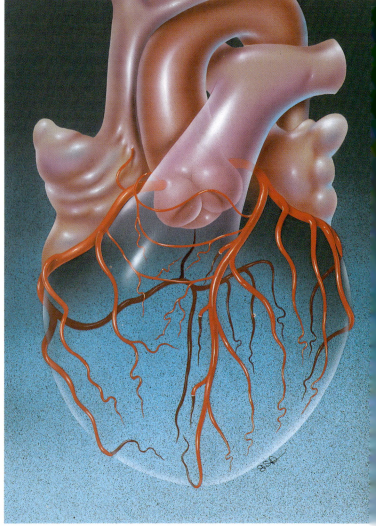

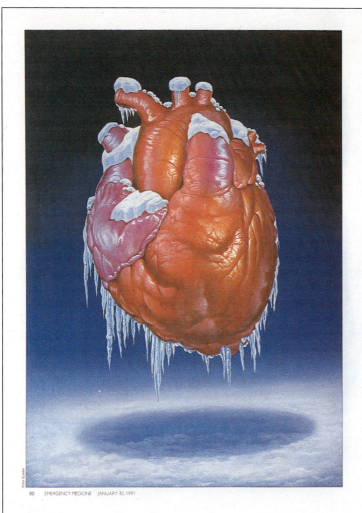

Title of Graphic: **Hypothermia and the Heart**
Client: **Emergency Medicine Magazine**
Art Director: **Lois Erlacher**
Illustrator: **Peter Scanlan**

Editorial

Title of Graphic: **Who, You? Malnourished? Good Bet**
Client: **Longevity**
Art Director: **Carveth Kramer**
Photographer: **John Uher**
Editor: **Rona Cherry**

Title of Graphic: **Herb: Just Another 4-Letter Word for Drug**
Client: **Longevity**
Art Director: **Carveth Kramer**
Photographer: **Yutaka Kawachi**
Editor: **Rona Cherry**

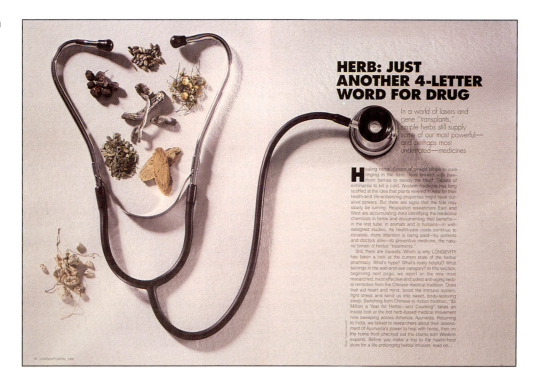

Editorial

Product: **Illustrated Medicine**
Title of Graphic: **Thrombolysis in Acute MI**
Design Firm: **Alexander & Turner**
Client: **ICI Pharma**
Art Director: **Edmond Alexander/Cynthia Turner**
Illustrator: **Edmond Alexander/Cynthia Turner**
Copywriter: **Nancy Agresta Weissflog**
Structural Designer: **Design/Type Inc./Larry Klein**

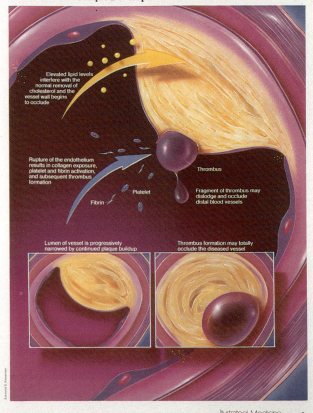

Editorial

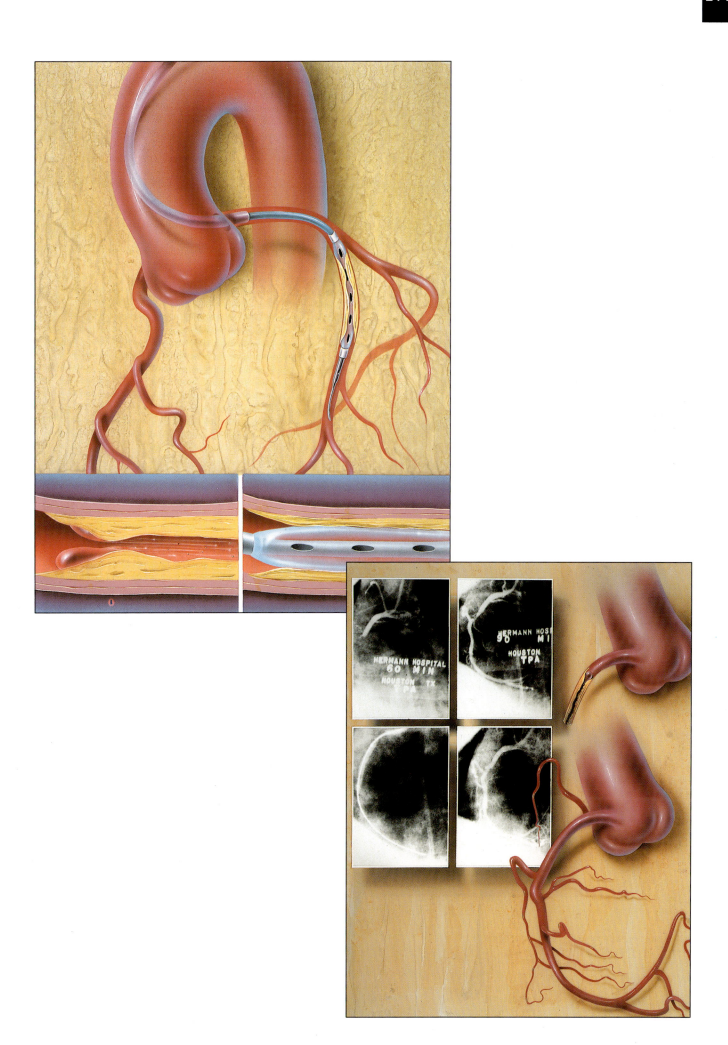

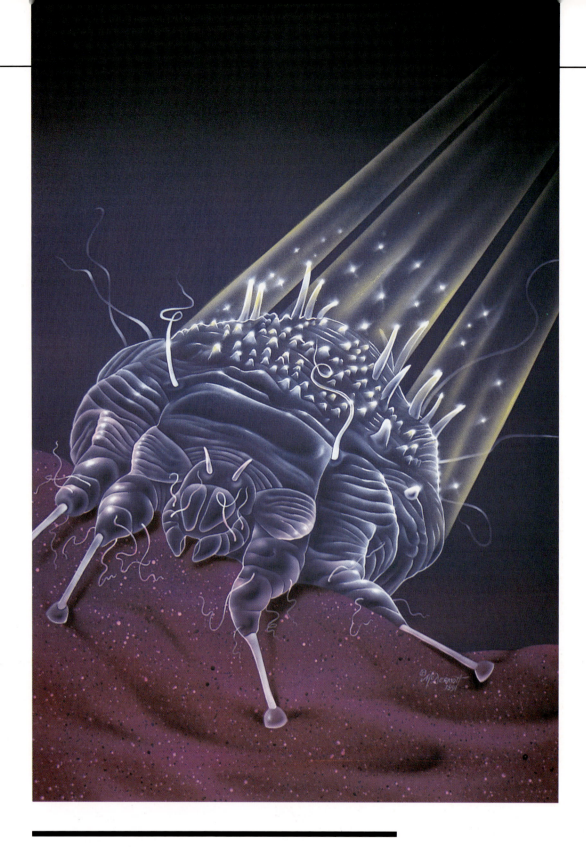

Title of Graphic: **Combating the Foes of the Feline Skin**
Client: **Veterinary Economics/Veterinary Medicine Magazine**
Art Director: **Mark Eisler**
Illustrator: **Teri J. McDermott**

Editorial

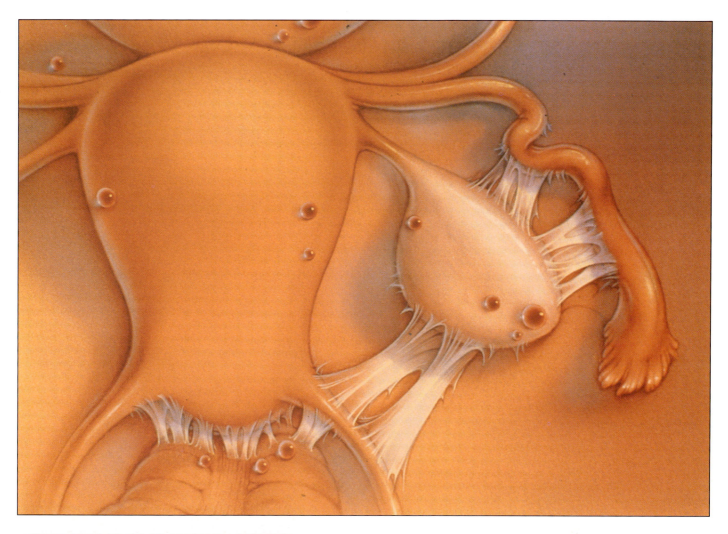

Product: **First Magazine**
Title of Graphic: **Endometriosis**
Client: **Bauer Publishing Company**
Art Director: **Rich Moscato**
Illustrator: **Lauren Keswick**

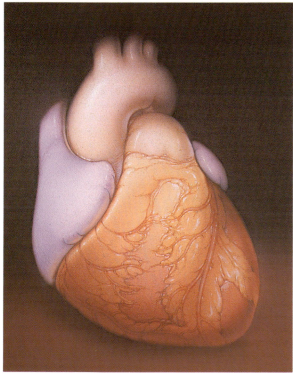

Product: **Longevity Magazine**
Title of Graphic: **Arrythmia**
Client: **Longevity**
Art Director: **Carveth Kramer**
Illustrator: **Lauren Keswick**

Editorial

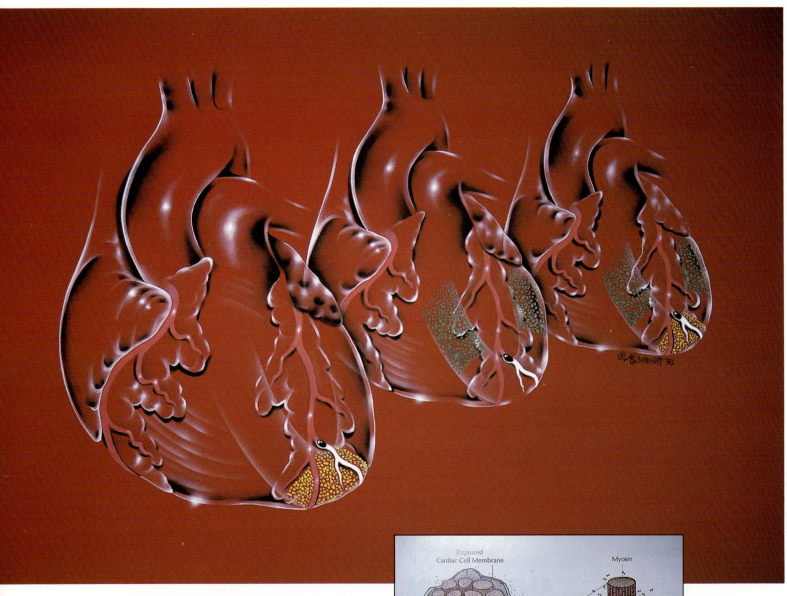

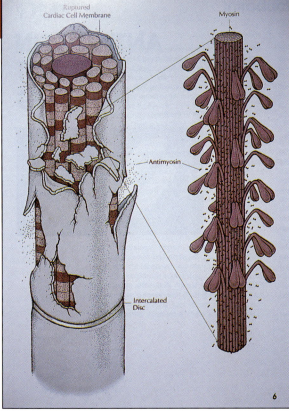

Title of Graphic: **New Imaging Approaches in Acute Coronary Artery Disease**
Design Firm: **H.P. Publishing Company**
Client: **Centocor, Inc.**
Art Director: **Robert S. Herald**
Illustrator: **Teri J. McDermott/Neil O. Hardy**
Copywriter: **Jean O'H. Fitzpatrick**
Structural Designer: **Robert S. Herald**

Editorial

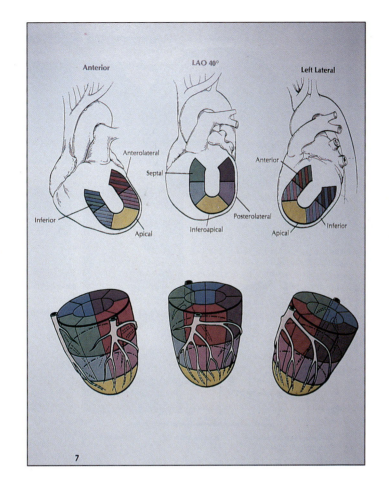

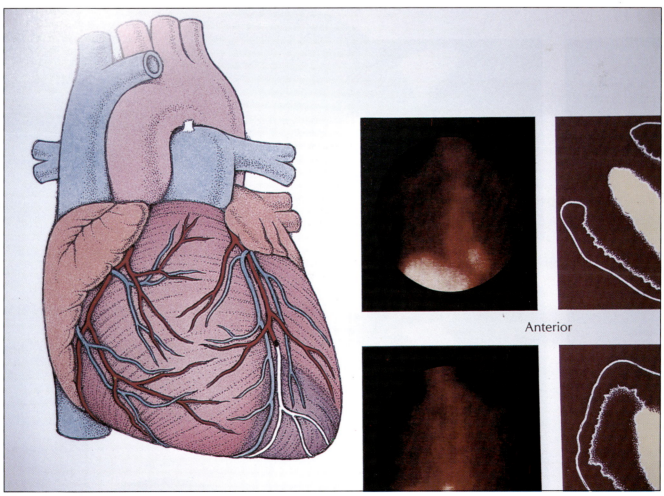

Editorial

216

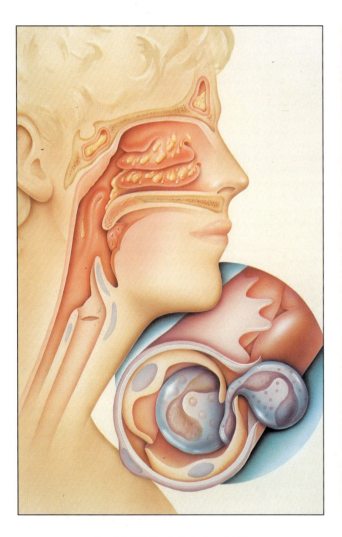

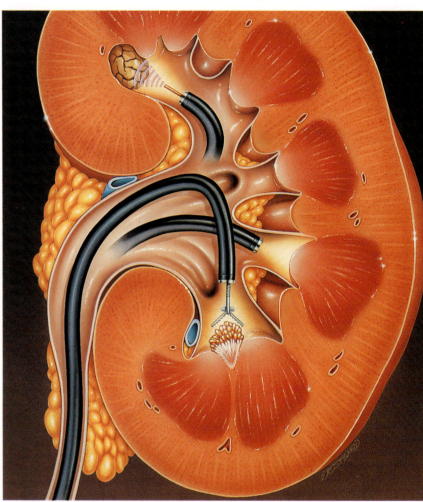

Title of Graphic: **Acute Sinusitis: Recognition and Response**
Ad Agency: **Etika Co. Ltd.**
Client: **Schering**
Art Director: **Jaime Jankelevich**
Illustrator: **Ellen Going-Jacobs**

Product: **Storz Ureteropyeloscope**
Title of Graphic: **New Ureteropyeloscope Offers Unmatched Capabilities**
Ad Agency: **Encore Direct Marketing**
Client: **Carl Storz**
Art Director: **Rich Fair**
Illustrator: **William B. Westwood**

Title of Graphic: **Total Knee System**
Design Firm: **Victor Skersis Graphic and Fine Arts**
Client: **Osteonics**
Art Director: **Christopher Beaudin**
Illustrator: **Victor Skersis**

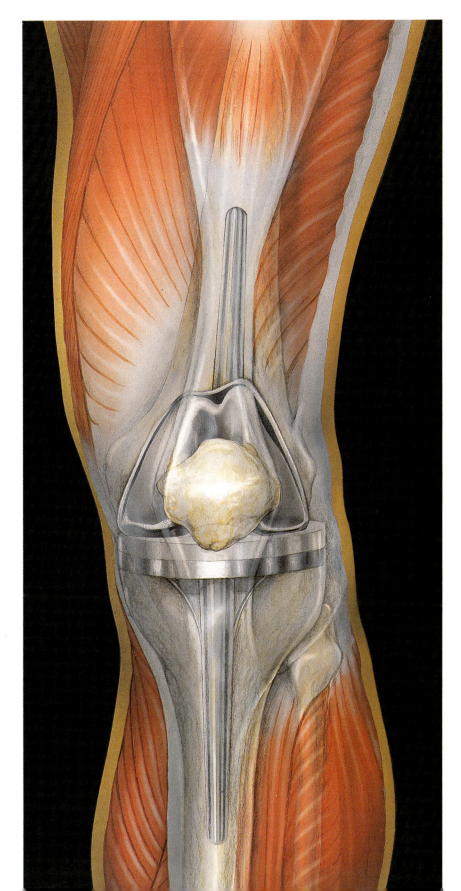

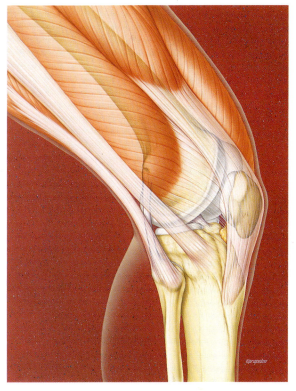

Product: **Bicycling Magazine**
Title of Graphic: **The Critical Joint**
Client: **Rodale Press**
Art Director: **John Pepper**
Illustrator: **John W. Karapelou**
Copywriter: **Nelson Pena**

Editorial

217

Editorial

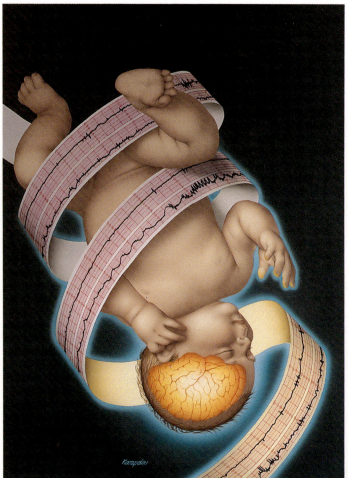

Product: **Contemporary Ob/Gyn Magazine**
Title of Graphic: **The Brain Damaged Baby**
Client: **Medical Economics Publishing Company**
Art Director: **A. Michael Velthaus**
Illustrator: **John W. Karapelou**

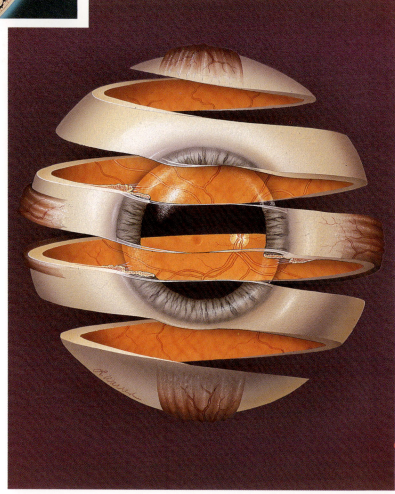

Product: **Opthalmology for the '90s**
Title of Graphic: **Cork Screw Eye**
Client: **UIC Eye Center**
Art Director: **Linda A. Warren**
Illustrator: **Linda A. Warren**

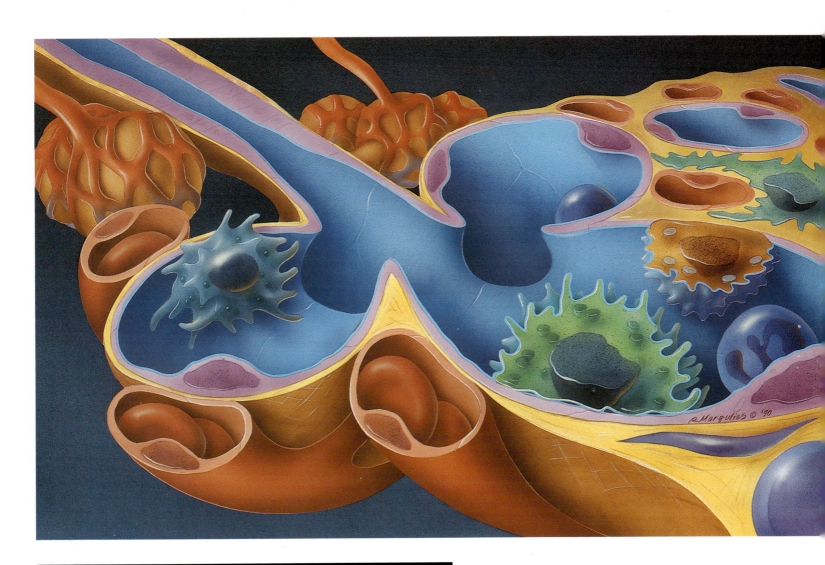

Title of Graphic: **Cellular and Spatial Environment of the Alveolar Macrophage**
Client: **Maclean Hunter Medical Communications Group, Inc.**
Art Director: **Robert Herald**
Illustrator: **Robert Margulies**

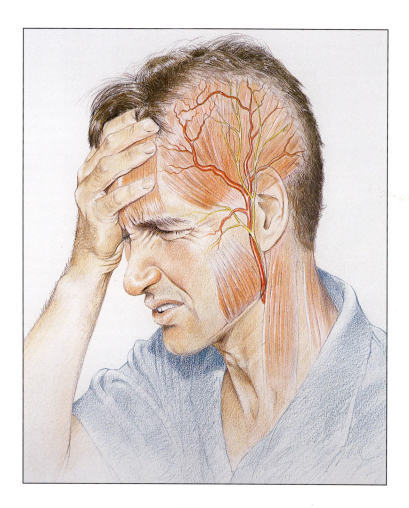

Product: **RN Magazine**
Title of Graphic: **The Most Common Types of Chronic Headache**
Client: **Medical Economics**
Art Director: **Anne Mattarella**
Illustrator: **Sharon Ellis**

Product: **Resident and Staff Physician**
Title of Graphic: **Tuberculosis in Children**
Client: **Romaine Pierson Publishers**
Art Director: **Anne Mattarella**
Illustrator: **Lauren Keswick**
Photographer: **Lauren Keswick**

Editorial

221

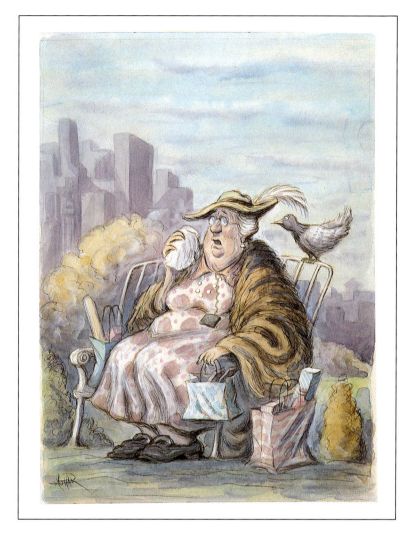

Title of Graphic: **Arrhythmias in Patients with CHF**
Client: **Postgraduate Medicine Magazine**
Art Director: **Tina Adamek**
Illustrator: **Brian Ajhar**

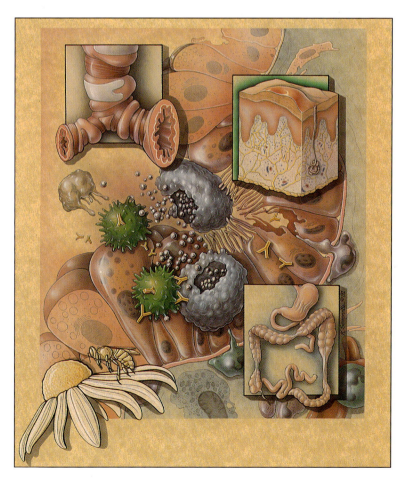

Product: **Patient Care Magazine**
Title of Graphic: **Anaphylaxis: The Mechanism and its Systemic Sequelae**
Client: **Medical Economics Publishing**
Art Director: **Nancy Stetler**
Illustrator: **Kevin A. Somerville**

Editorial

Title of Graphic: **Looking Beyond Convention**
Ad Agency: **Imagic**
Client: **Lederle Laboratories**
Art Director: **Daniel W. Smith**
Illustrator: **Hugh Syme**
Copywriter: **Frank Cordasco**

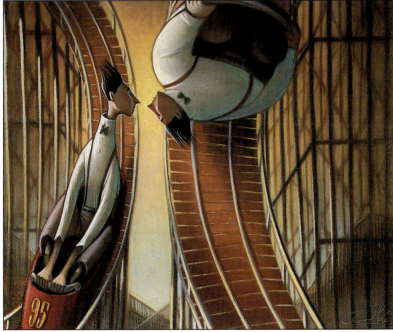

Title of Graphic: **Chronic Fatigue Syndrome: Is it Real?**
Client: **Postgraduate Medicine Magazine**
Art Director: **Tina Adamek**
Illustrator: **John Jude Palencar**

Title of Graphic: **The Risks of Riding the Weight-Loss Roller Coaster**
Client: **The Physician and Sportsmedicine Magazine**
Art Director: **Tina Adamek**
Illustrator: **Mary Grandpre**

Editorial

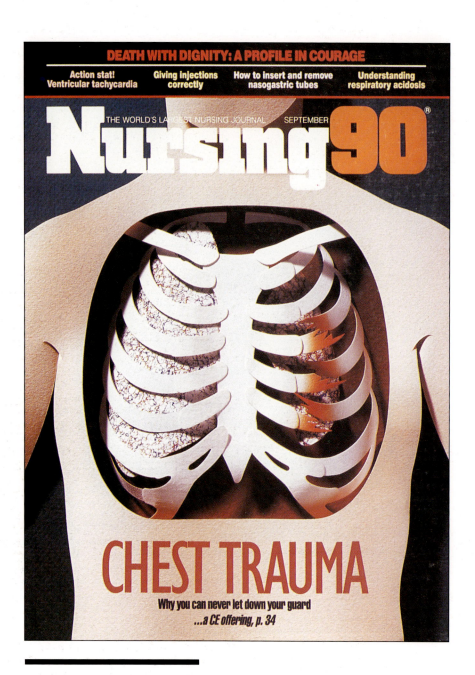

Product: **Nursing 90 Cover**
Title of Graphic: **Chest Trauma**
Art Director: **Ed Rosanio**
Illustrator: **Hal Lose**
Photographer: **Joel Zarska**

OTC/CONSUMER

The majority of this industry's target audience are the physicians, nurses, pharmacists, technicians, and other healthcare professionals — and yes, they are most definitely consumers. However, in the pharmaceutical/medical arena, consumer advertising is that area that promotes to any group that is *not* a healthcare professional. Two distinct areas exist within this industry: direct-to-the-consumer promotion of prescription products (which are highly regulated) and direct-to-consumer promotion of nonprescription products or services. Sometimes the promotion will inform. Sometimes it will educate. Sometimes it will compel, but like any other piece in this book, it is designed to sell.

OTC/Consumer

Product: **Lasix (furosemide)**
Title of Graphic: **With the Original Still at 16 cents, Generics aren't Worth the Change**
Ad Agency: **William Douglas McAdams, Inc.**
Client: **Hoechst-Rousell Pharmaceuticals, Inc.**
Art Director: **Patrick Creaven**
Phogtographer: **Murray Shear**
Copywriter: **Gwenne Freiman**

OTC/Consumer

Product: **Washington University Magazine Cover**
Title of Graphic: **Crossing the Genetic Trail**
Design Firm: **RCW Communication Design, Inc.**
Client: **Washington University Magazine**
Art Director: **Suzanne Oberholtzer & RCW Communication Design, Inc.**
Illustrator: **R.J. Shay**
Editor: **Cynthia Georges**

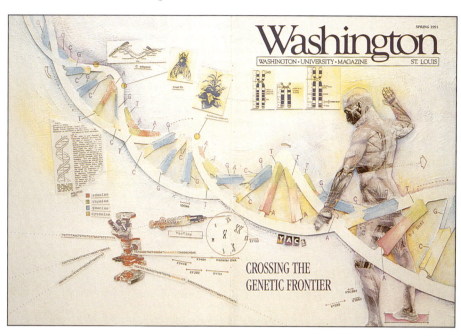

Product: **Vaseline Intensive Care Moisturizing Sun Block**
Title of Graphic: **Now, Make Every Sunny Day Safer**
Ad Agency: **Sudler & Hennessey**
Client: **Chesebrough Pond's, Inc.**
Art Director: **Joe Paumi**
Illustrator: **Joe Paumi**
Copywriter: **Elyn Raymon**
Structural Designer: **Packaging Trends**

OTC/Consumer

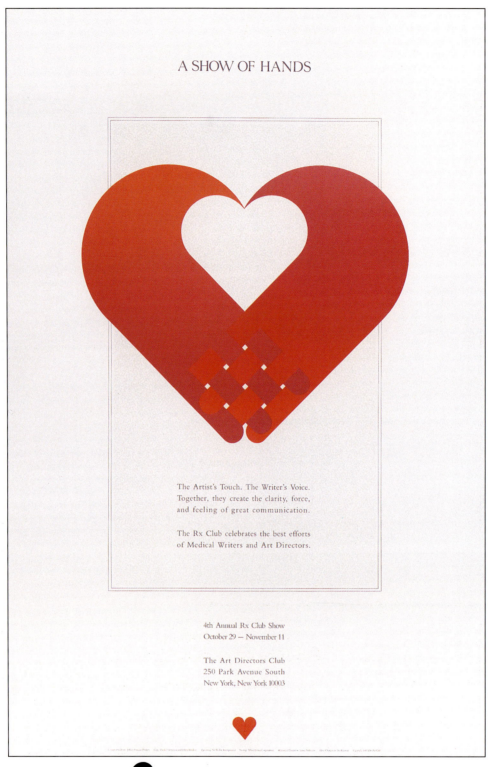

Product: **Rx Club**
Title of Graphic: **A Show of Hands**
Ad Agency: **KSP Communications**
Client: **Rx Club**
Art Director: **Jeffrey Pienkos**
Illustrator: **Susan Rickman**
Copywriter: **Jeffrey Pienkos/Daniel Sturtevant**

Product: **Rx Club**
Title of Graphic: **Rx**
Ad Agency: **KSP Communications**
Client: **Rx Club**
Art Director: **Jeffrey Pienkos**
Photographer: **William Wagner**
Copywriter: **Daniel Sturtevant**

OTC/Consumer

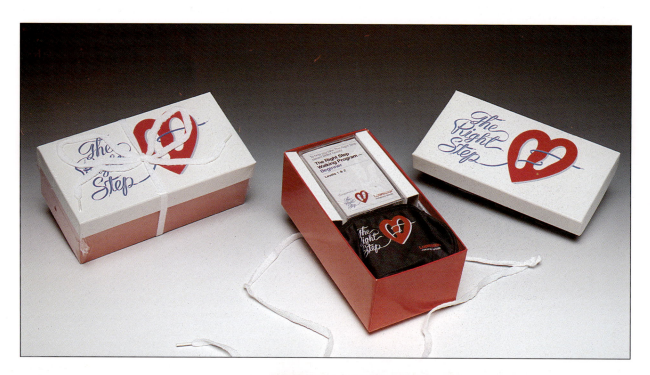

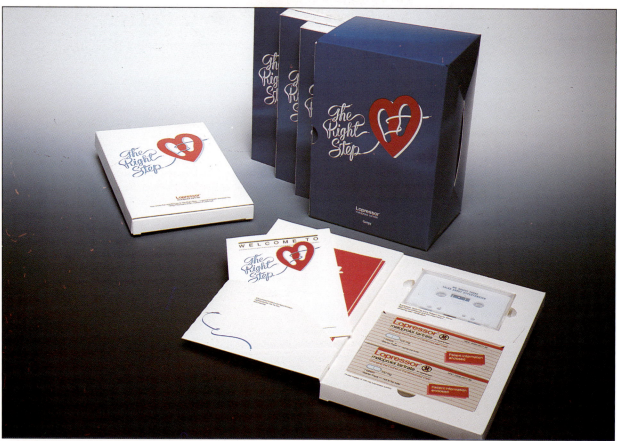

Product: **Lopresser**
Title of Graphic: **The Right Step**
Ad Agency: **C & G Advertising Agency, Inc.**
Client: **Ciba-Geigy Pharmaceuticals**
Art Director: **Loren Mork**
Illustrator: **Tom Carnase**
Copywriter: **Kevin Purcell**
Structural Designer: **Trimensions**

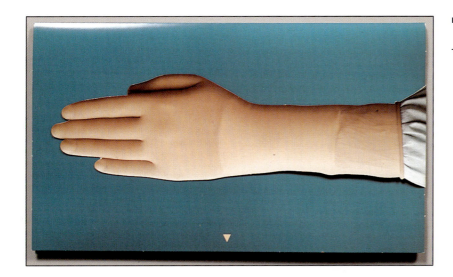

Product: **Neutralon Brown Surgical Gloves**
Title of Graphic: **Protection Inside, Protection Outside**
Design Firm: **Pierce-Davis & Associates**
Client: **Johnson & Johnson Medical, Inc.**
Art Director: **Pam Gampper**
Photographer: **Jim Buchanan**
Copywriter: **Pam Fields**

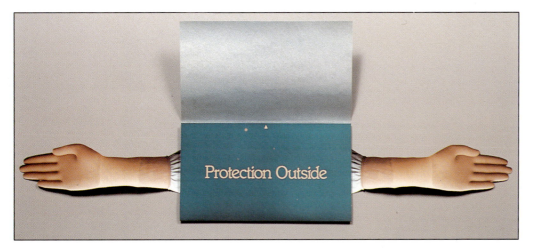

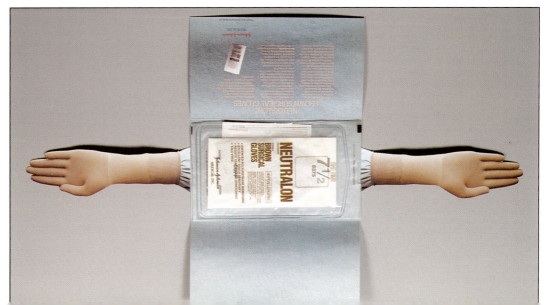

OTC/Consumer

Product: **Lopressor**
Title of Graphic: **The Right Step Patient Kit**
Ad Agency: **C & G Advertising**
Client: **Ciba-Geigy Pharmaceuticals**
Art Director: **Loren Mork**
Illustrator: **Tom Carnase**
Photographer: **Klesenski/Ward Photography**
Copywriter: **Kevin Purcell**
Structural Designer: **Packaging Co-ordinators**

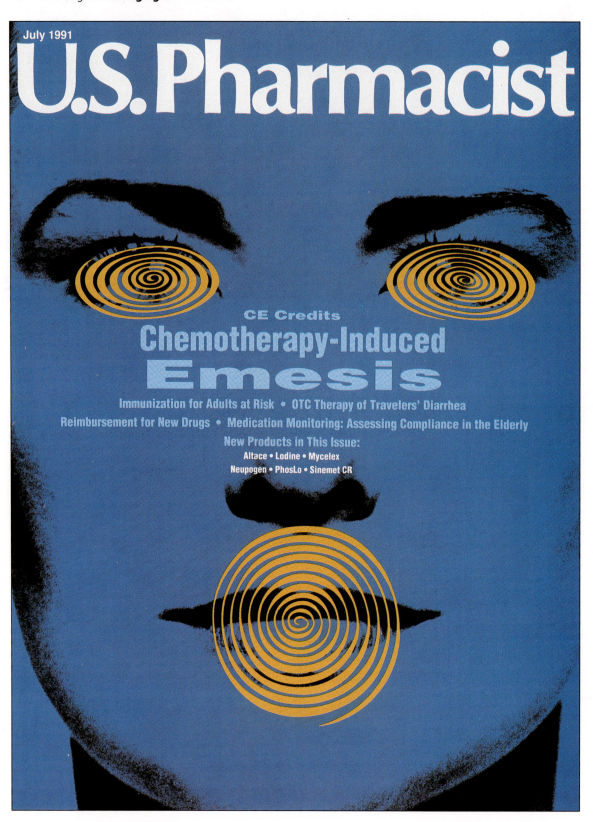

OTC/Consumer

Product: **Eldepryl**
Title of Graphic: **Eldepryl Direct Mail**
Ad Agency: **M.E.D. Communications**
Client: **Sandoz Pharmaceuticals Corp.**
Art Director: **Frank Kacmarsky**
Photographer: **Myron Jay Dorf**
Copywriter: **Nancy Sokasits**

ABOUT THE Rx CLUB SHOW

The Woman Behind the Scenes

Part Entrepreneur…
Part Agent…
Part Innovator…
Part Shrink…
Simply INA.
Pure delight.

Impressions of Ina Kramer are as varied as the roles she plays. Whether you need a source of information, a source of representation, or a source of inspiration — it's all as close as Ina herself. Since 1986 she has been responsible for founding two of the most innovative and highly regarded professional organizations in the field of medical/pharmaceutical advertising and publishing: The Art Director's Medical Survival Group and the Rx Club Show.

In 1982, Ina and family (and Gonzo the dog) relocated to San Francisco. There Ina met Ellen Going Jacobs, who was and still is employed at Krames Communications. This serendipitous combination of events was responsible for getting Ina started as a medical artists' representative.

As a graduate of the School of Visual Arts and with years of professional design experience, Ina had the eye to recognize talent. As the wife of an art director in the field of medical advertising and publishing, she was able to recognize a need.

As an entrepreneur, she was able to fill that need. Prior to The Art Director's Medical Survival Group, there was no comprehensive source for the type of top creative talent that understood the "art of medicine."

Ina became the first person to showcase the creative efforts of an entire industry dedicated to the art of medicine; in some instances, an industry with individuals whose creativity transforms medicine itself into an art form.

The History of the Rx Club Show

Like the Oscar, the Emmy, the Grammy, and the Tony (surely you remember the Clio), the Rx Club Show naturally evolved out the needs of an entire creative community to recognize and to be recognized by their own. But unlike those other creative awards, there was no prestigious organization or "academy" behind the first Rx Club Show — just an idea. The show was organized, the judges were recruited, the categories were developed, and the entries were solicited. Most importantly, the standards were set. The Rx Club Show was going to be judged solely on creativity — creative concept and execution were the only criteria for merit. Not media buy, not budget, just creativity.

The first show, held in 1986, included more than 1,800 creative entries from individuals, publications, and corporations. The judges for those first awards were 23 of the most prominent members in the fields of medical advertising and publishing, representing both copy and art. Since then, judges have included CEOs, all levels of VPs, Creative Directors, Associate Creative Directors, and senior-level creatives from both art and copy.

In the early years there were a few complaints from the writers that the Rx Show was an "art" show. It was the same old story: somebody had some white space and somebody else had a compelling need to fill it with words. There are two distinct thoughts on what makes effective printed communication. There are those who believe the picture's worth a thousand words, and there are those who believe that the right words can conjure up at least a thousand pictures. In 1989 the Rx Club developed an innovative award show for those who believed the pen (typewriter or word processor) was mightier than the marker — "The Best of The '80s Copy Show."

For the fifth show, the exhibition was held at the Ad Club in New York City and attracted a record number of viewers. Looking toward the future, the Rx Club Show will have 46 categories and will be expanding to include video submissions and entries from Europe.

On behalf of all of us who ever put pencil, marker, or ink (but especially blood, sweat, and tears) to paper, we'd like to extend our thanks to the Rx Club for their foresight and their fortitude.

The Judging

Judging for the annual Rx Club Show competition is conducted by a panel of experts from medical/pharmaceutical advertising and publishing from both the copy and art fields. The judges individually evaluate each entry and look for a strong concept, design originality, appropriate relationship between graphics and copy, as well as effective use of illustration, photography, and typography. The judges then consider how well all of the individual elements work together to achieve a successful creative solution and an effective communication.

After carefully considering all the entries, the judges assign a rating to each, using a numerical point system. Those pieces with the highest scores are selected to appear in the Rx Club Show. Entries with the overall highest numeric scores are the recipients of gold or silver awards. In recognition of the collaborative efforts involved, all persons responsible for creating each piece in the show (in addition to the advertising agency and the client company) receive an award.

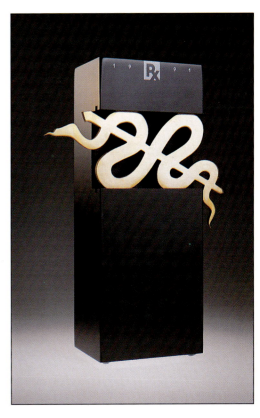

Information on Entering the Rx Club Show Competition

The entry deadline for the Rx Club Show competition varies each year, but the show itself is exhibited during the fall. In order for an entry to be eligible it must have been created or published within the twelve-month period preceding the entry deadline. For further information, contact The Rx Club, 61 Lexington Ave., Suite # 1H, New York, NY 10010. The phone number is 212.779.7632 and the fax number is 212.779.7635.

Text by Caren Spinner, San Rafael, California. A former Cardiovascular Technician and Physician's Assistant, Ms. Spinner has had many years of experience as an award-winning pharmaceutical copywriter, with both advertising and PR experience. In addition to copywriting, she has also had numerous magazine pieces published in the fields of fiction and nonfiction, was a ghostwriter for a book on orthopaedic medicine, and won an award for dramatic playwriting. She was formerly a judge for the American Academy of Radio Arts and Television Science's Emmy Awards in the categories of Daytime Drama and Children's Programming.

Print Categories

Magazine Advertising
1. Fractional Page
2. Full Page
3. Spread
4. Multiple Pages (insert R.O.B.)
5. Black and White
6. Campaign

Newspaper Advertising
7. Fractional Page
8. Full Page
9. Multiple Page (R.O.B. insert section or supplement)
10. Campaign

Direct Mail
11. Self-Mailer
12. Envelope Mailer
13. Campaign

Sales Promotion
14. Two-to-Four Page (visual/sales/detail aid)
15. More Than Four-Page (visual/sales/detail aid)
16. File Card
17. Booklet, Brochure
18. Patient Education Booklet
19. Single Sponsor Publication
20. Monograph, Trademark, Logo
21. Stationery
22. Self Promotion

Posters/Displays/Special Projects
23. Hospital Poster/Panel
24. P.O.P. Poster
25. Medical Office Poster
26. 3-D Models
27. Package Design
28. Premiums/Promotions
29. Public Service
30. Annual Reports

Editorial
31. Full-Page Color
32. Full-Page Black and White
33. Cover, Four-Color or Black/White
34. Consumer or Business Magazine (full issue)
35. Single Sponsor Publication

Medical Graphics Advertising/Editorial
36. Best Use of Illustration
37. Best Use of Photography
38. Non-Published Illustration
39. Non-Published Photography
40. Spot Illustration

OTC/Consumer
41. Magazine Advertising
42. Newspaper
43. Special Projects
44. Posters/P.O.P.
45. Package Design
46. Covers/Editorial

Video

Commercials
1. Up to 30 seconds
2. More than 30 seconds
3. Campaign (3 spots)

Public Service
4. Commercials
5. Campaign

Educational
6. Corporate
7. Corporate Series

Client Index

A.A.G.L., 182
Abbott Laboratories, 49, 74, 164
Abiomed Cardiovascular, Inc., 162
Adria Laboratories, Inc., 27, 172
Astra Pharmaceuticals, Inc., 65, 91

Bauer Publishing Co., 213
Beiersdorf, Inc., 53, 128, 130
Berlex Laboratories, Inc., 59
Boeringer Ingelheim Pharmaceuticals, Inc., 94, 98, 105
Braun, Inc./Oral-B Laboratories, 54
Bristol-Myers Squibb, 38, 64, 73, 104, 108
Burroughs Wellcome Co., 66
Business & Health, 196, 197

Caremark, 161
Carl Storz, 216
Centocor, Inc., 214
Chesebrough-Ponds, Inc., 101, 227
Ciba-Geigy Pharmaceuticals, 80, 87, 97, 103, 104, 137, 140, 141, 144, 167, 183, 230, 232
Connaught Laboratories, Inc., 60, 62
Contemporary Urology, 195
CPC International, 85

Datascope Corp., 88, 140, 186
Davis and Geck, 124
Dorritie Lyons & Nickel, 164
Drug Topics Magazine, 198

Eastman Kodak, 41
Elekta Instruments, Inc., 180
Eli Lilly and Co., 157
Emergency Medicine Magazine, 205, 208

Facial Prosthetics Clinic, 162
Fisons Pharmaceuticals, 43, 82, 123, 125

Geneva Marsam, 65

Glaxo Pharmaceuticals, Inc., 42, 122

Hoecsht-Roussell Pharmaceuticals, 37, 45, 102, 183, 226
Howard Hughes Medical Institute, 74

ICI Pharmaceuticals, 121, 202, 204, 210
Imagyn Medical, Inc., 161
Ina Kramer's Art Director's Medical Survivor's Group, 168

Janssen Pharmaceutica, 134
Johnson & Johnson Medical, Inc., 18, 63, 88, 147, 231

Kabia Pharmacia, Inc., 130
Keatings, 58
Keatings Pharmaceuticals, 61
Kinamed, Inc., 166
Knoll Pharmaceuticals, 108

Laboratories Recalcine S.A., 138
Lederle Laboratories, 80, 84, 95, 123, 167, 187, 222
Leo Medical, 59
LifeScan, Inc., 55
Lifetime Mecical Television, 170
Longevity, 192, 205, 209, 213

Maclean Hunter Medical Communications Group, Inc., 219
Marion Merrell Dow Pharmaceuticals Inc., 31, 48, 114, 173, 174, 176
McNeil Consumer Products Co., 106, 152
Medical Economics Publishing Co., 197, 218, 220, 221
Medical Laboratory Observer, 194
Medtronic, 26, 34, 148
Merck Sharp & Dohme International, 35, 131, 132, 138, 150, 153, 158, 189
Miles Inc., 115
Mills-Peninsula Hospitals, 160
MSD Agvet Division of Merck & Co., Inc., 49, 120, 122
Muro Pharmaceuticals, 20, 34
Mylan Pharmaceuticals, Inc., 52

National Livestock and Meat Board, 73
NJ Association for Biomedical Research, 165
The New York Times, 192
Norwich Eaton Pharmaceuticals, Inc., 31, 36
Nursing, 200, 201
Nycomed Imaging, 206

Ohmeda, 136
Oral-B Laboratories, 54, 69
Ortho Pharmaceutical Corp., 22, 48, 89, 97, 100
Osteonics, 217
Owen Galderma Laboratories, 98

PAC, 92
Parke-Davis, 19, 26, 27, 42, 66, 86, 136
Partnership for a Drug-Free America, 29, 76, 77
Patient Care Magazine, 196

Pfizer Pharmaceuticals, 21, 110, 112, 184
Physician and Sportsmedicine Magazine, 223
Pitman-Moore, Inc., 78
Postgraduate Medicine Magazine, 221, 223
Proctor & Gamble, Inc., 28, 33, 63, 82
Proworx, 117
Purdue Frederick Co., 37, 75, 101, 120

Q-Med, 21

Reckitt & Colman, 53, 103
Rhone-Poulenc Rorer, 33, 92, 107, 116
Rio Ethicals, 60
Roche Laboratories, 70, 71
Rodale Press, 217
Roerig, 145, 187
Romaine Pierson Publishing, 220
Rx Club, 93, 228, 229

Salthouse Torre & Norton, Inc., 163
Sandoz Pharmaceuticals, 39, 40, 45, 62, 67, 96, 233
Sanofi Diagnostics Pasteur, 124
Schering, 106, 118, 139, 155, 165, 216
Searle Laboratories, 67
Serono-Baker Diagnostics, 126
Shwarz Pharmaceutical Products, Inc., 189
Silor, 118
Smart Practice, 47
SmithKline Beecham Pharmaceuticals/The Upjohn Co., 72, 114, 146, 149, 151
Solvay, 32, 119, 144, 149
Storz Instrument Co., 188
Summit Pharmaceuticals, 141
Syntex, 24, 51, 71, 83, 102, 129, 154, 156, 190

Takeda USA, Inc., 44
Tap Pharmaceuticals, 81, 90
Terumo Corp., 143
3M Pharmaceuticals, 32, 36, 99, 107, 148

Toshiba American Medical Systems, 57

U.S. Pharmacist, 135
Upjohn, 58, 99, 117, 134
Ursapharm Arzneimittel GmbH, 46

Veterinary Medicine, 199, 212

Wallace Labs, 39
Warner Lambert Co., Inc, 50, 146
Washington University Magazine, 227
Weck Instruments, 142
Wesley-Jessen Corp., 166
Whitehall Laboratories, 43

Ad Agency / Design Firm Index

Abelson-Taylor, Inc., 90, 104, 114
Alexander & Turner, 202, 206, 210
Anatomical Chart Company, 188, 189
Art As Applied To Medicine/Johns Hopkins, 162

Barnum & Souza, Inc., 62, 98, 135
Bauer Publishing Co., 213
Baxter, Gurian and Mazzei, Inc., 47, 51, 83, 102, 154
Blunt Hann Sersen, Inc., 108, 124, 128, 130
Botto, Roessner, ome & Messinger, 22, 81, 89, 134, 152
Bryan Brown & Malinsky, 75

C & G Advertising Agency, Inc., 65, 80, 87, 141, 144, 165, 167, 183, 230, 232
Cline, Davis & Mann, Inc, 21, 117, 145, 170, 187

Dick Jackson, Inc., 88, 140, 186
Dorland Sweeney Jones, 104
Dorritie Lyons & Nickel, 21, 40, 110, 112, 164
Dugan/Farley Communications, 80, 97, 98, 105, 118, 172

Emergency Medicine Magazine, 205, 208
Encore Direct Marketing, 216
Esprit Communications, Inc., 160, 161
Etika Co. Ltd., 216

First Magazine, 213
Frank J. Corbett, Inc., 72, 73
Frederick & Valenzuela Ltda., 138

Gerbig Snell/Weisheimer & Associates, 74, 102, 147, 164

Girgenti, Hughes, Butler & McDowell, 20, 26, 32, 34, 36, 99, 107, 119, 148, 149
Grob & Co., Inc., 162
Gross Townsend Frank Hoffman, 64, 82, 94, 108, 153

H.P. Publishing Co., 214
Hal Lewis Group, 35, 129, 138, 150
Hall Decker McKibbin, Inc., 53, 128
Herald, Robert, 219
Howard Merrell & Partners, 78

Imagic, 222
Integrated Communications Corp., 45, 62

J. Walter Thompson Healthcare, 41, 76, 157
Jeffrey Pienkos Design, 93

Kallir, Philips, Ross, Inc., 42, 77, 97, 99, 100, 106, 116
Kasnot Medical Illustration, 204
Klemtner Advertising, 155
Koehler Iversen, Inc., 44
Kramer, Ina, 168
KSP Communications, 228, 229

Lally, McFarland & Pantello, Inc., 27, 28, 31, 33, 36, 85, 172
Lavey/Wolff/Swift, 66, 92, 115
The LeDA Agency, 84, 95, 123, 167, 187
Leverte Associates, Inc., 166, 169, 190
Lewis & Gace, Inc., 126, 174
Longevity Magazine, 192, 205, 208, 209, 213

M.E.D. Communications, 39, 40, 96, 167, 233
McCann Healthcare Advertising, 48, 173, 176

McCann-Erickson Manchester UK, 121
Medical Economics Publishing, 194, 195, 196, 197, 198, 218, 221
Medical Art, Inc., 154
Medicus Communications Ltd., 49, 103
MedPro Communications, Inc., 134
Merck, Sharp & Dohme International, 158

Nanos & Gray, Inc., 124
The New York Times, 192

Nursing, 200, 201

Patient Care Magazine, 196
Physician and Sportsmedicine Magazine, 223
Pierce-Davis & Associates, 18, 63, 88, 231
Plato Healthcare Promotions, 58, 59, 60, 61
Postgraduate Medicine Magazine, 221, 223
Pracon, 117, 118, 165, 166
Puches Design, Inc., 184

Radius Graphic Design, 182
Rainoldi Kerzner Radcliffe, 54, 55, 57, 69, 180
RCW Communications Design Inc., 74, 227
Rhone-Poulenc Rorer, 92
Rienzi & Rienzi Communications, Inc., 52
RN Magazine, 220
Rodale Press, 217
Romaine Pierson Publishers, 220
Rosner & Rubin, Inc., 136
RWR Advertising, Inc., 38, 39

Salthouse, Torre, Norton, 87, 114, 137, 144, 146, 149, 151, 163
Sandler Communications, 43, 82, 123, 125, 169
Simms & McIvor Marketing Communications, 142, 143
SMW Advertising, 30, 31, 38, 91
Sudler & Hennessey, 19, 26, 27, 29, 42, 43, 46, 59, 65, 66, 67, 77, 86, 101, 136, 227

Thomas G. Ferguson Associates, Inc., 45, 48, 49, 50, 107, 146
Trimensions, Inc., 103

Veterinary Medicine Publishing Co., 199, 212
Vicom/FCB, 24, 71, 131, 132, 156, 190
Victor Skersis Graphic and Fine Arts, 217

Warhaftig Associates, Inc., 120, 122, 151
William Douglas McAdams, Inc., 37, 70, 71, 101, 106, 120, 122, 139, 226